American English File

Third Edition

3

WORKBOOK

Christina Latham-Koenig
Clive Oxenden
Jerry Lambert

Paul Seligson and Clive Oxenden
are the original co-authors of
English File 1 and *English File 2*

OXFORD
UNIVERSITY PRESS

Contents

How to use your Workbook and Online Practice

American English File
Third Edition

Student Book

Use your Student Book in class with your teacher.

ACTIVITIES **AUDIO** **VIDEO** **RESOURCES**

Go to **americanenglishfileonline.com** and use the code on your Access Card to log into the Online Practice.

Workbook

Practice **Grammar**, **Vocabulary**, and **Pronunciation** for every lesson.

Online Practice

Look again at the Grammar, Vocabulary, and Pronunciation from the Student Book before you do the Workbook exercises.

Listen to the audio for the Pronunciation exercises.

Use the Sound Bank video to practice English sounds.

Practice the **Practical English** for every episode.

Watch the Practical English video before you do the exercises.

Use the interactive video for more Practical English practice.

Do the **Can you remember...?** exercises to check that you remember the Grammar, Vocabulary, and Pronunciation every two Files.

Look again at the Grammar, Vocabulary, and Pronunciation if you have any problems.

Practice Reading, Listening, Speaking, and Writing.

Anything is good if it's made of chocolate.
Jo Brand, British comedian

G simple present and continuous, action and nonaction verbs **V** food and cooking **P** vowel sounds

1 VOCABULARY food and cooking

a Circle the word that is different. Explain why.

1 peach chicken raspberries pear
The others are all *fruit*____.

2 chicken lamb squid beef
The others are all ____.

3 melon cherries peach cucumber
The others are all ____.

4 green beans beets cabbage duck
The others are all ____.

5 lemon salmon grapes cherries
The others are all ____.

6 zucchini crab mussels shrimp
The others are all ____.

b Match the words from the list to definitions 1–8.

avocado eggplant lobster mango
melon red pepper squid ~~tuna~~

1 a large sea fish that we eat
*tuna*____

2 a vegetable with dark purple skin
____

3 a tropical fruit with hard, dark green skin, soft, light green flesh, and a large seed inside
____

4 a sea animal with a soft body, eight arms, and two tentacles
____

5 a red vegetable that is empty inside
____

6 a tropical fruit, which has a yellow and red skin and is yellow inside
____

7 a sea creature with a hard shell and eight legs
____

8 a large round fruit with a thick yellow or green skin and a lot of seeds
____

c Label the pictures.

1 *grilled*____ salmon
2 ____ egg

3 ____ potato
4 ____ egg

5 ____ chicken
6 ____ peas

d Complete the sentences with a word from the list.

~~canned~~ fresh frozen low-fat raw spicy

1 We don't need *canned* tomatoes, we need fresh ones.
2 Are there any ____ peas in the freezer?
3 I don't like ____ fish, so I never eat sushi.
4 Hannah's on a diet, so she bought some ____ yogurt to have for dessert.
5 We buy ____ bread from the baker's every morning.
6 Mexican food can be very ____.

e Match the phrasal verbs in **bold** in questions 1–3 to definitions a–c.

1 Are there any food or drinks you'd like to **cut down on**? Which one(s)? _c_

2 Have you ever tried to **cut out** any food or drinks completely? Which one(s)? ____

3 Where do you usually go when you want to **eat out**? What do you usually have? ____

a to stop eating something completely

b to have lunch or dinner in a restaurant

c to eat less of something

f Answer the questions in **e**.

1 _____

2 _____

3 _____

VOCABULARY from listening

g Complete the sentences.

1 I m_iss_____ drinking good green tea when I go on vacation.

2 My favorite pizza t_____ are sausage and peppers.

3 I eat chocolate when I'm unhappy to ch_____ myself u_____.

4 We sometimes eat r_____-m_____ food for dinner when we get home from work late.

5 I'm a_____ to peaches, so I never eat them.

6 Do you ever get t_____-o_____ food from the Chinese restaurant on the corner?

7 I don't like tuna as a sandwich f_____.

2 PRONUNCIATION vowel sounds

a Write the words in the chart.

beef   carton   chicken   chocolate   cookie
crab   fork   jar   mango   lobster   peach   pork
squid   sugar   tuna   zucchini

1 fish	2 tree	3 cat	4 car
	beef		

5 clock	6 horse	7 bull	8 boot

b 🔊 1.1 Listen and check. Then listen again and repeat the words.

c Write the words.

1 /bɔɪld/   _boiled_____

2 /ˈkæbɪdʒ/   _____

3 /ˈspaɪsi/   _____

4 /roʊstɪd/   _____

5 /greɪps/   _____

6 /frut/   _____

7 /beɪkt/   _____

8 /ˈmɛlən/   _____

9 /ˈɛgplænt/   _____

d 🔊 1.2 Listen and check. Then listen again and repeat the words.

3 GRAMMAR simple present and continuous, action and nonaction verbs

a Complete the sentences with the simple present or continuous form of the verbs in parentheses.

1 I sometimes _feel_ tired after lunch. (feel)

2 We _____ usually _____ late on the weekend. (not get up)

3 _____ you _____ the TV or can I turn it off? (watch)

4 My boss _____ to work every morning. (walk)

5 Can you call back later – I can't hear you. We _____ a party, and the music is very loud. (have)

6 There's a man in our neighbors' yard. What _____ he _____? (do)

7 How often _____ your teacher _____ you homework? (give)

8 I _____ chocolate this month. I need to cut down on sweet things. (not eat)

9 My mother _____ often _____ yoga. (not do)

10 My friend has stopped eating snacks. He _____ to be healthier. (try)

b Correct any mistakes in the highlighted phrases. Check (✔) the correct sentences.

1 I like your jacket. Is it new?   ✔

2 Something is smelling good. What are you making? ✘
  Something smells good.

3 That cake is looking delicious. Did you make it?
  _____

4 I don't know what to cook for dinner.
  _____

5 Are you thinking the fish is cooked now?
  _____

6 Can I call you back? I'm having lunch right now.
  _____

7 This soup tastes very spicy. What's in it?
  _____

8 I'm loving all kinds of vegetables. There aren't any I don't eat.
  _____

c Complete the sentences using the correct form of a verb from the list.

believe   not belong   ~~drive~~   play   not recognize
not sleep   sound   not use

1 I can't talk now, I'_m driving_. I'll call you when I get to the office.

2 I think your boyfriend is telling the truth – I _____ him.

3 Can you turn off your computer if you _____ it?

4 This bag _____ to me. Is it yours?

5 Sarah isn't home. She _____ tennis.

6 I'm tired because I _____ well right now.

7 I _____ that woman. Do you know who she is?

8 That music _____ awful. Would you mind turning it down?

d Write questions.

1 what / you / do right now
  What are you doing right now ?

2 where / you / usually do your homework
  _____ ?

3 why / you / study English
  _____ ?

4 you / think English is easy
  _____ ?

5 you / enjoy the classes right now
  _____ ?

6 what / you / usually do after the class
  _____ ?

e Write an email to your teacher. Use the questions in **d** to help you.

> ✉
>
> Hi _____,
>
> _Right now, I'm doing my English homework._
> _____
> _____
> _____
> _____
> _____
>
> Hope you're well.
>
> Best wishes,
>
> _____

🔄 **Go online** for more practice

Happy families are all alike; every unhappy family is unhappy in its own way.
First line of Anna Karenina
by Leo Tolstoy, Russian writer

G future forms: present continuous, *be going to, will / won't* | **V** family, adjectives of personality | **P** sentence stress, word stress

1 VOCABULARY family, adjectives of personality

a Complete the sentences with a family word.

1 Your mother and father are your p<u>arents</u>.
2 Your grandfather's father is your
   gr_____-gr_____.
3 A child who has no brothers or sisters is an
   o_____ ch_____.
4 Your brother's or sister's daughter is your
   n_____.
5 A child who parents take into their family and treat as
   their own is an a_____ ch_____.
6 Your partner, children, parents, and brothers and
   sisters are your i_____ family.
7 Your father's new wife is your st_____.
8 Your wife or husband's brother is your
   br_____-i_____-l_____.
9 A sister who shares one parent with you is your
   h_____-s_____.
10 Your brothers and sisters are your s_____.
11 Your grandparents, aunts, uncles, and cousins are
   your e_____ family.
12 Your brother's or sister's son is your n_____.
13 Your stepmother's or stepfather's daughter from an
   earlier relationship is your st_____.

b Match the comments to the personality adjectives from the list.

ambitious   anxious   honest   independent
insecure   patient   rebellious   self-confident
selfish   sensible   ~~spoiled~~   stubborn

1 "When I want something, my parents always give it to
   me."
   <u>spoiled</u>
2 "I find it very hard to relax. Sometimes I lie awake at
   night for hours worrying about things."
   _____
3 "There aren't any cookies left for you. I was hungry, so
   I ate them all."
   _____
4 "I'm going to go to bed early so I can sleep well
   before my exam tomorrow."
   _____
5 "I feel very comfortable when I'm speaking in public."
   _____
6 "I'd like to be the manager of a big multinational
   company."
   _____
7 "That's what I think, and I'm not going to change my
   mind."
   _____
8 "I'd prefer to do this on my own, thanks."
   _____
9 "I was a really difficult teenager. I didn't obey any
   rules at school or home."
   _____
10 "Take your time. I can wait. I'm not in a hurry."
   _____
11 "Excuse me. You dropped some money. Here it is."
   _____
12 "I'm not sure if Jess is my friend or not. She says she
   is, but I don't really know."
   _____

c Read the sentences and complete the crossword with the missing adjectives.

Crossword grid with:
- 1 Down starts with C H A R M I N G
- across/down cells for numbers 2, 3, 4, 5, 6, 7, 8, 9

DOWN ↓

1 Omar's attractive, friendly, and ▓▓ – everybody loves him!
2 Naomi's really ▓▓. She loves going out, and she has a lot of friends.
3 My niece is very ▓▓ for her age – you'd never guess she was only 12.
4 Laura's very ▓▓ – she writes some wonderful stories.
7 Laila's so ▓▓. She's always telling other people what to do.

ACROSS →

3 My boss is really ▓▓. Sometimes he's fine, but other times he gets angry about the smallest thing.
5 It isn't fun playing tennis with my brother because he's so ▓▓. He hates losing.
6 I'm lucky to have a friend like Paul because he's very ▓▓. He's always there when I need his help.
8 My grandma's very ▓▓. She loves us all very much, and she gives us lots of hugs and kisses.
9 It's very easy to make Sofia cry because she's very ▓▓.

d Write the opposite adjectives. Use a negative prefix.

1 clean   *unclean*
2 honest   _____
3 mature   _____
4 reliable   _____
5 sensitive   _____
6 ambitious   _____
7 imaginative   _____
8 organized   _____
9 responsible   _____
10 sociable   _____
11 friendly   _____
12 kind   _____
13 patient   _____
14 selfish   _____

e Complete the sentences with *sensible*, *sensitive*, or *sympathetic*.

1 Don't be so _____! I didn't mean to make you cry.
2 Be _____! There are only three three extra spaces in our car. We can't take the whole soccer team home!
3 Be _____! Her hamster died, and she's very upset!

2 GRAMMAR future forms

a Complete the sentences with the correct form of the verbs or phrases in **bold**.

1 **he / look for** (an intention)
My brother hates his job.
He's going to look for a new one.

2 **I / pay** (an offer)
Don't worry about the drinks.
_____ for them.

3 **I / make** (an offer)
_____ some more coffee.

4 **you / get married** (a prediction)
Do you think _____ before you're 30?

5 **we / go** (an arrangement)
_____ on vacation tomorrow.
I can't wait!

6 **I / have** (an instant decision)
A Are you ready to order?
B Yes, _____ the steak.

7 **I / be** (a fact)
_____ 21 on my next birthday.

8 **we / meet** (an arrangement)
_____ your parents for a meal this weekend.

9 **I / not be** (a promise)
I'm going to Maria's house for dinner, but I _____ home late.

10 **it / break** (a prediction)
There are too many groceries in this bag.
I think _____.

b Complete the conversations with the correct future form of the verbs in parentheses.

1 A _Are_____ you _going away_____ this weekend? (go away)
  B No, we _____ here. Why? (stay)
  A We _____ a barbecue. Would you like to come? (have)

2 A I'm too tired to cook. I _____ Chinese take-out. (order)
  B Good idea. I _____ the restaurant. What do you want for your appetizer? (call)
  A I _____ spring rolls, please. (have)

3 A What time _____ you _____ this morning? (leave)
  B I _____ the six o'clock train. (get)
  A I _____ you a ride to the train station, then. (give)

4 A What _____ you _____ tonight? (do)
  B I _____ to the movies with some friends. (go)
  A What movie _____ you _____? (see)
  B The new *Star Wars* movie.
  A Oh, I've seen it. You _____ it! (love)

5 A I _____ you do the dishes. (help)
  B OK. I _____ and you can dry. But please be careful with the glasses. (wash)
  A Don't worry. I _____ anything! (not break)

c Answer the questions. Use the correct future forms.

1 What are you going to do after the class?
  First, I'm going to go shopping.
  Then, I'm going to go home and make dinner.

2 What do you think the weather will be like tomorrow?
  In the morning, it _____.
  In the afternoon, I think it _____.

3 What are you doing this weekend?
  I _____.

4 What are your plans for next summer?
  I _____.

3 PRONUNCIATION sentence stress

a 🔊 1.3 Listen and complete the sentences.

1 _When_____ are you going to _book_____ your _vacation_____?
2 I'm _____ going to _____ the _____.
3 I'm going to _____.
4 _____ are you _____?
5 I'm _____ some _____.
6 I'm _____ my _____.
7 She's _____ her _____.
8 _____ will you _____ your _____?
9 I _____ them _____.
10 I'll _____ them on _____.

b 🔊 1.3 Listen again and repeat. Copy the rhythm.

Go online for more practice   Go online to check your progress   9

Practical English Meeting the parents

reacting to what people say

1 REACTING TO WHAT PEOPLE SAY

a Circle the correct answers. ONE or TWO answers may be correct.

1 **A** Kate's going to study abroad for a year!
B *What a great idea!* / *Oh, no!* / *What a pity.*

2 **A** I left my wallet at home again!
B *How fantastic!* / *I don't believe it.* / *You're kidding.*

3 **A** I didn't get the job.
B *That's great news!* / *What a pity.* / *Never mind.*

4 **A** We're getting married!
B *How fantastic!* / *That's great news!* / *Oh, no!*

5 **A** Dave bought a new car.
B *Never mind.* / *Really?* / *What a pity.*

6 **A** I lost my phone.
B *Oh, no!* / *How fantastic!* / *That's great news!*

b Complete the chart with the correct phrases from **a**.

1 Reacting to something surprising
I don't believe it!
_____

2 Reacting to something interesting
_____

3 Reacting to some good news
_____
_____
_____

4 Reacting to some bad news
_____
_____
_____

2 HOW + ADJECTIVE, WHAT + NOUN

Complete the phrases with *How* or *What*.

1 *How* _____ interesting!
2 _____ a good idea!
3 _____ terrible news!
4 _____ awful!
5 _____ amazing!
6 _____ a pity!

3 SOCIAL ENGLISH

Complete the conversations with the phrases from the list.

_____

a really nice guy   Go ahead   How do you see
How incredible   I mean   Not really   That's because
things like that

1 **A** What do you think of Isabel's new boyfriend?
B He's *a really nice guy* .

2 **A** _____ your life in ten years?
B I think I'll be married and have my own company.

3 **A** I hear you're an excellent swimmer. Would you like to be a professional?
B _____. I don't have enough time to train.

4 **A** I'm sorry. I'm not feeling hungry.
B _____ you ate too much for lunch!

5 **A** You know, I think we went to the same school.
B _____! What a coincidence!

6 **A** Can I have another piece of chicken, please?
B _____. There's more in the kitchen.

7 **A** What kinds of books do you read?
B Biographies, historical fiction, _____.

8 **A** Would you like to come to the concert with us?
B No, sorry. _____, I'd love to, but I'm busy.

Go online to practice the Practical English phrases

Can you remember...? 1

1 GRAMMAR

Complete the sentences.

1 Excuse me. The ticket office is closed. What time _____ it _____ ?

2 Tony's in his room. He _____ _____ his homework.

3 Sorry, I _____ with you. I think you're wrong.

4 _____ you _____ a suit to the wedding next Saturday?

5 We _____ a barbecue on Friday. Would you like to come?

6 Don't worry. I promise I _____ home late tonight.

2 VOCABULARY

Circle the word that is different.

1 crab   duck   lobster   squid
2 beef   chicken   lamb   salmon
3 stepsister   niece   nephew   half-sister
4 aunt   uncle   cousin   mother
5 affectionate   bossy   honest   patient
6 charming   moody   selfish   stubborn

3 PRONUNCIATION

Circle the word with a different sound.

🐟	fish	1 grilled siblings reliable squid
🌳	tree	2 beef great niece steamed
🐱	cat	3 anxious family imaginative mature
🚗	car	4 carton charming father jar
🐴	horse	5 four organized pork spoiled

4 GRAMMAR & VOCABULARY

Read the article. Circle a, b, or c.

CHANGING EATING HABITS

Eating habits [1]_____ healthier, according to the results of a government survey. The study [2]_____ the food bought by the average family over the last 40 years. One of the greatest differences is the type of milk that people are drinking. Today, many [3]_____ buy skimmed milk rather than full-fat milk for their families. This is probably because of campaigns to help people [4]_____ the amount of fat they eat. Another type of food that contains less fat and is very popular today is oven French fries. These are French fries that are [5]_____ in the oven without adding fat. It [6]_____ that people today are also more adventurous in what they eat. Instead of frozen fish, they're now buying more fresh seafood, such as shrimp and [7]_____. As for meat, people are eating less [8]_____ and lamb, and more chicken and ground beef. Italian food is extremely popular today and [9]_____ pasta is available in supermarkets, as well as the cheaper dried version. In general, nutritionists are happy with the results of the survey and hope that people [10]_____ eating healthily in the future.

1	**a** are becoming	**b** become	**c** is becoming
2	**a** compare	**b** is comparing	**c** compares
3	**a** nephews	**b** parents	**c** siblings
4	**a** cut down on	**b** cut down	**c** eat out
5	**a** baked	**b** boiled	**c** steamed
6	**a** is seeming	**b** seem	**c** seems
7	**a** cherries	**b** grapes	**c** mussels
8	**a** lobster	**b** peach	**c** pork
9	**a** fresh	**b** grilled	**c** raw
10	**a** continues	**b** is continuing	**c** will continue

✓ **Go online** to check your progress

2A Spending money

present perfect and simple past **V** money **P** o and or

When a man tells you he got rich through hard work, ask him "Whose?"
Don Marquis, US Writer

1 VOCABULARY money

a Complete the sentences with the correct verb in parentheses.

1 My sister *wastes* a lot of money on clothes she never wears. (wastes / saves)
2 I can't _____ to buy a house of my own. (pay / afford)
3 You'll have to _____ a lot of money if you want to travel around the world next year. (save / waste)
4 We still _____ the bank a lot of money. (owe / earn)
5 Ji-sung _____ about $2,000 a month at his new job. (raises / earns)
6 That painting _____ a lot of money. (charges / is worth)
7 My uncle is doing a bike ride to _____ money for charity. (afford / raise)
8 I don't want to lose these earrings. They _____ a fortune! (cost / owed)
9 I'll have to _____ some money from the bank if I want to buy a new car. (borrow / lend)
10 Mary _____ $10,000 from her grandfather when he died. (inherited / invested)
11 I _____ $5,000 in a company, and I made a 5% profit. (inherited / invested)
12 The plumber _____ me $300 to fix my shower. (cost / charged)
13 Can you _____ me $200 until I get paid? (borrow / lend)

b Complete the sentences with the correct preposition.

1 I'll pay *for* the meal if you get the drinks.
2 They charged us $10 _____ a bottle of water.
3 My friends got _____ debt when they bought their new house.
4 We borrowed some money _____ my parents.
5 Rena puts all her extra money _____ the bank.
6 I don't mind lending money _____ people in my family.
7 Andy and Sue spent a lot of money _____ their son's education.
8 Can I pay _____ credit card?
9 If I lend you some money, when can you pay me _____?
10 Phil invested all his money _____ his own company.

c Complete the advertisement with the words from the list.

~~bills~~ budget contactless payment loan mortgage salary tax

What's so good about WIN-WIN Bank?

WIN-WIN Bank provides all the traditional banking services while using the latest technology.

What's new

Use our **WIN-WIN** phone app to manage your money and pay your ¹ *bills*. For extra convenience, sign up for ² _____ and you'll never have to carry cash with you again.

What hasn't changed

Need money for a car or a vacation? We'll give you a ³ _____ of up to $10,000 for whatever you want to buy. If you're buying a house, we can give you a ⁴ _____ at one of the lowest interest rates on the market.

Someone to talk to

Finding it hard to get to the end of the month? Our advisors can help you plan a ⁵ _____ to make your money go farther. If you're working, they can give you advice on how to manage your ⁶ _____ each month and how much ⁷ _____ you should be paying.

So, if you're looking for a new bank, just remember: **WIN-WIN** has it all!

Online Banking
Customer ID
Password
LOGIN

12

d Complete the questions with a phrasal verb from the list.

live off   live on   pay back   ~~take out~~

1 How often do you use an ATM? How much money do you usually _take out___?
2 When was the last time you lent money to somebody? How long did it take them to _____ you _____?
3 Why do young people sometimes _____ their parents?
4 What's the smallest amount of money you think you could _____ for a month? What would you spend it on?

e Answer the questions in **d**.

1 _____
2 _____
3 _____
4 _____

VOCABULARY from reading

f Complete the compound nouns in the sentences.

1 We use olive o_il_ for all our cooking.
2 Max fell off his bike during our bike tr_____, but he didn't hurt himself.
3 Becky doesn't use beauty tr_____ that are tested on animals.
4 Our electricity b_____ is going to be very high this month – we've had the heat on every day.
5 I usually drink tap w_____ with my meals.
6 I try to buy environmentally-friendly cleaning pr_____ because they don't pollute the water.

2 PRONUNCIATION *o* and *or*

a Circle the word with a different sound.

⬆ up	1 m**o**ney n**o**thing (s**o**rry) w**o**n
🕐 clock	2 c**o**ntactless sh**o**pping d**o**llar cl**o**thes
☎ phone	3 **o**we d**o**ne s**o**ld l**o**an

b 🔊 2.1 Listen and check. Then listen again and repeat the words.

c Look at the pairs of words. Is the pronunciation of *or* the same (S) or different (D)?

1 aff**or**d   **or**ganized   _S_
2 st**or**e   w**or**se   _D_
3 m**or**tgage   f**or**k   ____
4 sh**or**t   w**or**k   ____
5 w**or**ld   w**or**th   ____
6 **or**der   w**or**d   ____

d 🔊 2.2 Listen and check. Then listen again and repeat the words.

3 GRAMMAR present perfect and simple past

a Circle the correct answer.

1 *I've never owed* / *never owed* any money to the bank in my life.
2 Rachel wants to buy a house, but she *hasn't saved* / *didn't save* enough money yet.
3 They've *charged* / *charged* us too much for our meal last night.
4 Paul *hasn't inherited* / *didn't inherit* anything from his grandmother when she died.
5 I can't pay you back. I *haven't been* / *didn't go* to the ATM yet.
6 *I've never used* / *never used* contactless payment, but I'd like to try it.
7 How much *has your TV cost* / *did your TV cost*?
8 I *haven't had* / *didn't have* any coins, so I couldn't put any money in the parking meter.
9 I love your house – how long *have you lived* / *did you live* in it?
10 My girlfriend has a really well-paid job. She *has earned* / *earned* $85,000 last year.

b Complete the conversations with the correct form of the verbs in parentheses.

1 A When _did_ your son _buy_ his car? (buy)
   B When he _____ his driver's test last month. (pass)

2 A How much money _____ you _____ from your sister yesterday? (borrow)
   B About $100, but I _____ _____ it already. (spend)

3 A _____ you _____ a new apartment yet? (find)
   B Yes, and the bank _____ _____ to give me a mortgage. (agree)

4 A _____ you ever _____ any money to a friend? (lend)
   B Only to my boyfriend when he _____ a new phone. (need)

5 A _____ your mother _____ an appointment with the doctor yet? (make)
   B Yes, she _____ him yesterday, and she's seeing him tomorrow. (call)

c Re-order the words to write present perfect and simple past questions.

1 **a** you / buy a house
       Have you ever bought a house?
   b when / you / buy it
       When did you buy it?

2 **a** you / find any money on the street
       _____?
   b how much / you / find
       _____?

3 **a** you / use contactless payment
       _____?
   b where / use it
       _____?

4 **a** you / pay for a meal for a lot of people
       _____?
   b why / you / pay for it
       _____?

5 **a** you / stay in an expensive hotel
       _____?
   b who / you / stay there with
       _____?

6 **a** you / raise money for charity
       _____?
   b how much / you / raise
       _____?

d Answer the questions in **c**.

1 **a** _____
   b _____
2 **a** _____
   b _____
3 **a** _____
   b _____
4 **a** _____
   b _____
5 **a** _____
   b _____
6 **a** _____
   b _____

Go online for more practice

Only I can change my life.
No one else can do it for me.
Carol Burnett, US actress & comedienne

G present perfect + *for / since*, present perfect continuous   **V** strong adjectives: *exhausted, amazed,* etc.   **P** sentence stress

1 GRAMMAR present perfect + *for / since*, present perfect continuous

a Write the words and phrases from the list in the correct column.

~~2015~~   a long time   December
I was very young   lunchtime   six months
two weeks   three days   Tuesday   years

for	since
	2015

b Complete the sentences with the present perfect simple form of the verb in parentheses and *for* or *since*.

1 I *'ve had* _____ my car *for* about a month. (have)

2 My mom _____ sick _____ weeks. (be)

3 We _____ each other _____ we were in college. (know)

4 Owen _____ for the same company _____ five years. (work)

5 Dan and Vicky _____ in Boston _____ they got married. (live)

6 My parents _____ gardening _____ they were young. (love)

7 I _____ to go to Australia _____ a long time. (want)

8 Lola _____ to me _____ last year. (not speak)

9 I _____ my grandparents _____ a long time. (not see)

10 Max _____ Ayesha _____ they were in school together. (like)

c Complete the conversations with the present perfect continuous form of the verbs.

1 A Did you know that Amy's in a band?
  B No. *Have they been playing* together for a long time? (they / play)

2 A How long was your flight?
  B Twelve hours. _____ all day. (we / travel)

3 A My brother has a very good job in New York.
  B Really? How long _____ there? (he / work)

4 A Diana has finally moved into a new apartment.
  B Oh good! _____ one for a long time. (she / look for)

5 A Why does Marco's teacher want to see you?
  B _____ his homework lately. (he / not do)

6 A You're late.
  B Yes, I know. Sorry. _____ long? (you / wait)

7 A You look exhausted.
  B _____ the kids all day! (I / look after)

8 A How's your soccer team doing, Pete?
  B Pretty good, but _____ recently. I hurt my foot. (I / not play)

d Circle the correct form. If both forms are possible, check (✔) the sentence.

1 How long *have you lived / have you been living* abroad? ✔

2 *I've studied / I've been studying* Chinese for two years. ◻

3 My parents *have had / have been having* the same car for ten years. ◻

4 How long *has Mark played / has Mark been playing* the bass guitar? ◻

5 Alex *has worked / has been working* in this school since he started teaching. ◻

6 *I've known / I've been knowing* her for years. ◻

7 *We've gone / We've been going* to the same dentist since we were children. ◻

8 *You've worn / You've been wearing* the same coat for years! ◻

9 How long *have you ridden / have you been riding* horses? ◻

10 *I've washed / I've been washing* the car; it looks much cleaner now. ◻

e What have you been doing recently? Write five sentences. Use the ideas from the list or your own ideas.

> a book   a hobby   a job   a new habit   a sport   a TV show
> your work / studies

I've been eating more vegetables because I want to be healthier.
I have exams, so I've been studying.

1 _____
2 _____
3 _____
4 _____
5 _____

2 PRONUNCIATION sentence stress

a ◐ 2.3 Listen and complete the sentences.

1 I've been *traveling all day* _____.

2 _____ have they
been _____?

3 She's been _____ since _____.

4 They _____ been _____
for _____.

5 We've been _____ the _____
_____.

6 I _____ been _____.

b ◐ 2.3 Listen again and repeat the sentences. Copy the rhythm.

3 VOCABULARY strong adjectives

a Match the regular adjectives 1–14 to the strong adjectives a–n.

1 tired	*d*	a	amazed
2 surprised	___	b	boiling
3 big	___	c	delighted
4 cold	___	d	exhausted
5 dirty	___	e	filthy
6 funny	___	f	freezing
7 happy	___	g	furious
8 hot	___	h	fascinating
9 hungry	___	i	hilarious
10 interesting	___	j	huge
11 small	___	k	positive
12 sure	___	l	starving
13 afraid	___	m	terrified
14 angry	___	n	tiny

b Complete the sentences with the strong adjectives from **a**.

1 The couple is _delighted_.

2 They're _____.

3 It's really _____.

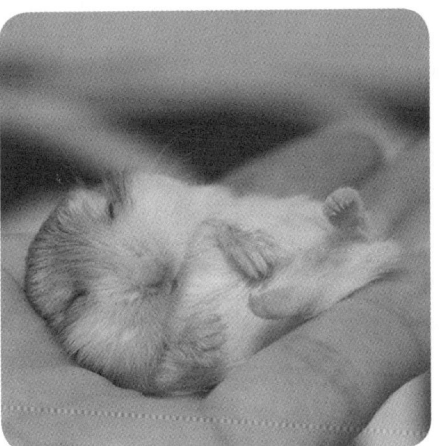

4 He's _____.

5 It's a _____ hamster.

6 She's absolutely _____.

c Complete the sentences with the strong adjectives from **a**.

1 The temperature has been going up all week, and now it's absolutely _boiling_.

2 I'm _____ that you don't know the name of the president of the US.

3 Tom's parents have just found out he's been missing school, so they're _____.

4 I've been watching a horror movie, and now I'm absolutely _____.

5 We're _____ because we've hiked 8 miles today.

6 That movie is _____! We laughed all the way through it.

7 This book is _____. I've learned so much from it.

8 I've been thinking about your question, and now I'm _____ I know the answer.

d Complete the sentences about you.

1 The last time I had a huge meal was when _____ _____.

2 The weather was absolutely boiling when I _____ _____.

3 One of the most hilarious movies I've seen is _____ _____.

4 I felt really exhausted when I _____ _____.

5 When I'm absolutely starving, the thing I most want to eat is _____.

6 I was delighted with a present I got _____ _____.

7 I saw a fascinating TV show recently about _____ _____.

8 Something that makes me furious is _____ _____.

Go online for more practice   Go online to check your progress

3A Survive the drive

A good traveler has no fixed plans.
Lao Tzu, Taoist Philosopher

G choosing between comparatives and superlatives | **V** transportation | **P** /ʃ/, /dʒ/, and /tʃ/, linking

1 VOCABULARY transportation

a Complete the crossword.

DOWN ↓   ACROSS →

1 M
O
T
2 O
R
3 C
Y
4 C
5 L   6
E

7
8

b Complete the compound nouns with one word.

1 Don't forget to put your _seat_____ belt on.

2 You'll get a _____ ticket if you leave your car there.

3 Sorry we're late. There was a terrible _____ jam downtown.

4 The trip took us twice as long because there was _____ work on the freeway.

5 I wish bike riders would use the _____ lane instead of the sidewalk.

6 We need to fill up at the _____ station before we leave.

7 The traffic is always worse during _____ hour.

8 There wasn't anybody waiting at the taxi _____.

9 Slow down! There are _____ cameras on this road.

10 We had to stop at the traffic _____ because it was red.

11 There was a terrible _____ crash, so they closed the freeway.

12 This road is dangerous to cross. Let's use the _____ walk.

13 Do you know what the speed _____ is on this road?

14 They made this street a _____ zone, so there aren't any cars.

c Complete the sentences with the correct form of *take*.

1 It usually *takes* two hours to get to my mother's house.
2 How long _____ it _____ to get downtown on a weekday?
3 It usually _____ us about 45 minutes to get to the airport.
4 It _____ me two hours to get to work yesterday.
5 I'm not looking forward to driving to Los Angeles tomorrow. It _____ about eight hours to get there.
6 How long _____ it _____ you to get home last night?

d Complete the sentences with the words from the list.

| off (x2)   out   out of   up (x2) |

1 We asked our neighbor to drop us *off* at the airport.
2 They set _____ early because they wanted to arrive before lunch.
3 Charlie forgot his GPS, so he ended _____ getting completely lost.
4 Look _____! That car isn't going to stop.
5 Do you think you could pick me _____ from the train station?
6 I ran _____ gas because I forgot to fill up when I left home.

e Answer the questions.

1 How do you usually travel around your town or city?
_____
2 How do you usually travel when you go on vacation?
_____
3 What's the traffic like during rush hour where you live?
_____
4 What's the speed limit on the freeway in your country?
_____
5 How long does it take you to get downtown?
_____
6 Who usually picks you up and drops you off at the airport?
_____
7 Have you ever run out of gas? If so, where were you going?
_____
8 Have you ever gotten lost? If so, where did you end up?
_____

2 PRONUNCIATION /ʃ/, /dʒ/, and /tʃ/

a Circle the word with a different sound.

dʒ jazz	1 bri**dge** **cheap** **j**ourney mortga**ge**
ʃ shower	2 **sh**ation cra**sh** wa**tch** ru**sh**
tʃ chess	3 ca**tch** **j**am adventure coa**ch**

b ◆ 3.1 Listen and check. Then listen again and repeat the words.

3 GRAMMAR choosing between comparatives and superlatives

a Write sentences with the information from the survey. Use the comparative or the superlative.

Where to go?

We reveal the results from our reader survey of three popular vacation destinations.

	Bangkok (Thailand)	Dubai (UAE)	Cancun (Mexico)
It's expensive	★	★★★	★★
It's crowded	★★★	★★	★★
It's easy to get to	★★	★★	★★★
It's exciting	★★★	★★	★★
It's hot	★★	★★★	★★
It's relaxing	★	★★	★★★

1 Dubai / expensive / Bangkok
   Dubai is more expensive than Bangkok.

2 Bangkok / crowded of the three destinations

   _____

3 Cancun / easy to get to / Bangkok

   _____

4 Bangkok / exciting / Dubai

   _____

5 Dubai / hot / Cancun

   _____

6 Cancun / relaxing of the three destinations

   _____

b Complete the sentences with one word.

1 Gas isn't as expensive in the US *as* _____ it is in the UK.
2 My father drives more slowly _____ my mother.
3 This is _____ cheapest gas station in the city.
4 Let's go by train. It's _____ comfortable than the bus.
5 This is the _____ day of my life – everything has gone wrong!
6 I think trains are _____ dangerous than cars. There are fewer accidents.
7 It's _____ to go by subway than by bus. Buses are much slower.
8 Singapore is the _____ expensive city in the world.
9 You're at the Sheraton? We're staying at the same hotel _____ you.
10 Why don't we walk? It's the _____ expensive way to travel.

c Complete the second sentence so it has a similar meaning to the first sentence. Use the word in parentheses. Write 3–5 words. Contractions are two words, e.g., *isn't*.

1 My apartment is bigger than my boyfriend's. (big)
   My boyfriend's apartment *isn't as big as* mine.
2 You don't walk as fast as me. (than)
   I _____ you.
3 I've never been to a more interesting city than Istanbul. (most)
   Istanbul is _____ I've been to.
4 My job isn't as interesting as yours. (less)
   My job _____ yours.
5 I've never eaten a better pizza. (the)
   This is _____ I've ever eaten.
6 The train is more expensive than the bus. (as)
   The bus _____ the train.
7 We have the same car. (as)
   Your car _____ mine.
8 I've never slept in such an uncomfortable bed before. (least)
   That's _____ I've ever slept in.

4 PRONUNCIATION linking

a ◀ 3.2 Listen and complete the sentences.

1 It's the *most dangerous* _____ thing I've ever done.
2 It's _____ going by train than by bus.
3 The _____ place to visit is the museum.
4 Flying is a lot _____ than going by train.
5 Scooters aren't _____ motorcycles.
6 It's the _____ I've been here.

b ◀ 3.2 Listen again and repeat the sentences. Listen carefully to the linked words. Copy the rhythm.

 Go online for more practice

3B Men, women, and children

Men want to be a woman's first love. Women like to be a man's last romance.
Oscar Wilde, Irish writer

G articles: *a / an, the,* no article **V** collocation: verbs / adjectives + prepositions **P** /ə/, two pronunciations of *the*

1 GRAMMAR articles

a Circle the correct words.

1 Yesterday was *hottest / the hottest* day of the year so far.
2 We went to New York City for my birthday *last weekend / the last weekend.*
3 I think *girls / the girls* are better at learning *languages / the languages* than *boys / the boys.*
4 Did you lock *door / the door* when you left *house / the house* this morning?
5 My sister works for *Japanese / a Japanese* company. She's *engineer / an engineer.*
6 I don't usually like *fish / the fish,* but *salmon / the salmon* we had last night was delicious.
7 We go to *movies / the movies* once *a week / the week.*
8 Don't worry! It's not *the end / end* of *the world / world.*
9 Do you think *women / the women* are more sensitive than *men / the men?*
10 What *beautiful day / a beautiful day!* Let's have *lunch / a lunch* on the patio.

b Correct any mistakes in the highlighted phrases. Check (✔) the correct sentences.

1 That's pretty dress – the color suits you.   ✗
   a pretty dress

2 He's going to visit his parents the next weekend.

3 The money doesn't make people happy.

4 My grandfather left school when he was 14.

5 I go to the dentist about twice a year.

6 Have you worn jacket that you bought last week?

7 That was one of the best meals I've ever had.

8 What noisy child! Where are his parents?

9 Alex is studying to become doctor.

10 I love cats, but my boyfriend doesn't like them.

11 Her husband sits in front of the TV all day.

12 She always leaves the work at five thirty.

c Complete the text with *a / an*, *the*, or – (no article).

DNA
the reason women see colors better than men

Why are women generally able to see [1]_____ colors better than men? Scientists say there is [2]_____ reason for this, and [3]_____ reason is in our DNA. Our chromosomes contain DNA, which controls many things about us. The ability to see [4]_____ color red is carried by the X chromosome. Men have only one X chromosome, but [5]_____ women have two of them. This means that it's easier for women to see red. This was important in prehistoric times when women were looking for [6]_____ fruit to eat. They needed to choose [7]_____ right fruit, so they had to be able to see [8]_____ difference between different colors. If they made [9]_____ mistake, they could kill their families and themselves. So, it was more important for women to see different colors, while men had [10]_____ other important skills.

2 PRONUNCIATION /ə/, two pronunciations of *the*

a 🔊 3.3 Listen and complete the sentences.

1 *I'd like*_____ to *speak*_____ to the *manager*_____.
2 The bus is _____
   _____ train.
3 What are we going _____
   _____ ?
4 Could you open _____
   _____?
5 She needs _____
   _____ her ankle.
6 We want _____
   _____ tomorrow.

b 🔊 3.3 Listen again and repeat.

c 🔊 3.4 Listen and repeat the phrases. Pay attention to the pronunciation of *the*.

1 The conversation was about the woman next door.
2 The university invited a guest to speak at the meeting.
3 I sometimes go to the theater in the evening.
4 We took the elevator instead of walking up the stairs.
5 The office gave me all the information I needed.
6 The gray skirt is nice, but I prefer the black one.

3 VOCABULARY collocation

a (Circle) the correct prepositions.

1 They're arriving *at* / *on* / (*in*) Seoul on Friday.
2 That suitcase belongs *for* / *from* / *to* me.
3 Let's ask someone *at* / *for* / *of* directions.
4 We might go camping, but it depends *in* / *of* / *on* the weather.
5 Everybody laughed *about* / *at* / *to* Zach when he fell off the chair.
6 Who's going to pay *for* / *of* / *with* the meal?
7 I dreamed *about* / *from* / *with* my old school friends last night.
8 That girl reminds me *about* / *of* / *to* my cousin.
9 I apologized *at* / *to* / *with* the teacher *about* / *for* / *of* being late.
10 He often argues *at* / *to* / *with* his friends about politics.
11 We arrive *at* / *in* / *to* Union Station in Denver at 7:45.
12 She doesn't believe *about* / *in* / *on* ghosts.
13 I can't choose *between* / *of* / *with* the green one or the blue one.
14 They're really looking forward *for* / *of* / *to* their vacation.
15 James spends a lot of money *for* / *in* / *on* expensive presents for his girlfriend.

b Complete the sentences with the correct preposition.

1 I'm tired *of* my job. I think it's time for a change.
2 My boyfriend isn't very passionate _____ soccer.
3 He's famous _____ his role in *Sherlock Holmes*.
4 I'm not very interested _____ abstract art.
5 Nina is very different _____ her sister.
6 Adam's very good _____ math.
7 I'm fed up _____ this gray weather.
8 My brother is very worried _____ his daughter right now.
9 A lot of people are scared _____ spiders.
10 They're angry _____ their son _____ his terrible exam grades.
11 She's very close _____ her brother.
12 My husband is very proud _____ his new car.
13 I'm very fond _____ my grandfather. He's a wonderful person.
14 Experts say that walking is good _____ you.
15 Jack's older brother isn't very nice _____ him.
16 We're really happy _____ our new sofa.
17 The children are very excited _____ going to the concert.
18 My neighbor was very rude _____ me yesterday.
19 Gus used to be married _____ Maya.

4 PRONUNCIATION when are prepositions stressed?

a 🔊 3.5 Listen and complete the conversations.

1 A Who did you *argue with* _____?
  B I _____ with my _____.

2 A Who are you _____?
  B I'm _____ at _____!

3 A What are you so _____?
  B I'm _____ about my _____.

4 A What are you _____?
  B I'm _____ to the _____.

b 🔊 3.5 Listen again and repeat. <u>C</u>opy the <u>rhy</u>thm.

🔄 **Go online** for more practice   ✅ **Go online** to check your progress

Practical English A difficult celebrity

giving opinions

1 GIVING OPINIONS

a Match sentences 1–9 to responses a–i.

1 Do you like reggae? __f__
2 What do you think of Ed Sheeran? ____
3 Do you still listen to your old CDs? ____
4 I've heard that musicians make a lot of money. ____
5 I'd love to be famous! ____
6 Classical music is great for a quiet meal. ____
7 What's your opinion of heavy metal? ____
8 What kind of music does your girlfriend like? ____
9 Do you like this band? ____

a I agree. You can listen to it and talk to each other at the same time.
b To be honest, I haven't asked her.
c Sometimes. But it's easier listening to a music streaming service. Don't you agree?
d No, they're terrible. What do you think?
e I don't think that's right. Only a few of them earn enough to live on.
f It's OK. But if you ask me, rap is more fun.
g I like him. But in my opinion, Bruno Mars is better.
h Oh sure, it would be great to start with. But you'd soon get fed up with all the photographers.
i Personally, I think it's a little loud.

b Complete the conversations with the highlighted phrases from **a**. Use each phrase once only.

1 A What do you think of music festivals?
   B They're OK. *But in my opinion*, there are too many people.
   A Yes, you're right.

2 A Do you think Cathy has a good voice?
   B _____, I've never heard her sing.
   A Well, you should!

3 A Do you ever listen to the radio?
   B Not really. The DJs talk too much. _____?
   A Yes, they do.

4 A For me, the 80s was the best decade for music.
   B _____, the 80s were good, but there's been some great music since then, too.
   A I suppose so.

5 A Do you like this song?
   B Not really. _____?
   A It's awful.

6 A Do you like live music?
   B Yes, I do. _____, it's a little expensive.
   A Absolutely!

7 A People shouldn't listen to loud music on public transportation.
   B _____. They should wear headphones.
   A That's right.

8 A Jazz music started in the UK.
   B _____. I'm pretty sure it began in the US.
   A Of course it did! Sorry about that.

9 A What's your opinion of Rihanna's new song?
   B _____ it's better than the last one.
   A Me too.

2 SOCIAL ENGLISH

Complete the conversations with a phrase from the list.

Hang on a minute   It's just that my boyfriend's away
~~That's so kind of you~~   You've come back
Did you mean what you said

1 A I brought you some flowers.
   B Thank you. *That's so kind of you.*

2 A _____.
   B Yes, I forgot my phone.

3 A _____ about moving abroad?
   B No, of course I didn't. I was only kidding.

4 A You look upset. What's the matter?
   B Nothing really. _____ and I miss him.

5 A I'm going out for a walk. Do you want to come?
   B _____. I'll get my coat.

Go online to practice the Practical English phrases

Can you remember...? 1–3

1 GRAMMAR

Complete the sentences with one word.

1 I _____ need a new car right now. My old car works perfectly.
2 That suitcase looks heavy. I _____ get a cart for you.
3 I'm not ready to go. I haven't put on my coat _____.
4 I've been learning English _____ three years.
5 Your cooking is _____ than mine – this tuna is delicious!
6 My sister's studying medicine. She wants to be _____ doctor.

2 VOCABULARY

Circle the word that is different.

1 beets cabbage grapes green beans
2 charming mature sociable spoiled
3 borrow loan owe save
4 angry furious starving terrified
5 train truck motorcycle van
6 fond of fed up with passionate about pleased with

3 PRONUNCIATION

Circle the word with a different sound.

↑ up	1 done gone money nothing	
clock	2 fond lobster watch worry	
phone	3 cost sold owe roasted	
shower	4 adventure ambitious crash sociable	
chess	5 catch charming peach machine	

4 GRAMMAR & VOCABULARY

Read the article. Circle a, b, or c.

Jobs for women

Kerry Cassidy is one of Britain's 19,000 train drivers. She [1]____ a train for eight years now, and she's very happy with her job. The situation for women train drivers has changed a lot [2]____ 1978 when Karen Harrison became the first in the UK. At that time, the male drivers were generally not very nice [3]____ women.

Today, the job is [4]____ for women to do than it was in the past because attitudes have changed. One of [5]____ things about it is the salary. Georgiana Oana [6]____ a train driver for a year. She [7]____ £55,000 a year, so she's been able to get a [8]____ to buy her own house. Kerry Cassidy is a single mother, but she can easily [9]____ childcare for her two children while she's away at work. Kerry believes there is nothing about being [10]____ that makes it a man's job. She says that there is no reason why women shouldn't apply.

	a	b	c
1	drives	is driving	has been driving
2	for	from	since
3	at	to	with
4	easier	easiest	more easy
5	better	best	the best
6	has been	is	was
7	costs	earns	wins
8	bargain	budget	mortgage
9	afford	charge	raise
10	train driver	a train driver	the train driver

✓ Go online to check your progress

4A Bad manners?

> When a man opens the car door for his wife, it's either a new car or a new wife.
> *Duke of Edinburgh, husband of Queen Elizabeth II*

G obligation and prohibition: *have to, must, should* **V** phone language **P** silent consonants

1 VOCABULARY phone language

a Match the words from the list to definitions 1–12.

busy   call back   cut somebody off   dial   go off
hang up   leave a message   put somebody on hold
ringtone   swipe   ~~text / message~~   voicemail

1 to send somebody a message using a cell phone
text / message

2 to make a caller wait until the person they want to talk to is free
_____

3 to call somebody again or call somebody who called you earlier
_____

4 to start ringing
_____

5 to record information for somebody to listen to later
_____

6 an electronic system that can store messages so that you can listen to them later
_____

7 to stop or interrupt somebody's phone conversation
_____

8 to push the buttons on a phone to call a number
_____

9 the sound your phone makes when somebody is calling you
_____

10 to move content across a screen using your finger
_____

11 meaning that a phone is in use and can't be called
_____

12 to end a phone conversation and put the phone down
_____

b Complete the sentences with the words from **a**.

1 I wanted to speak to my boss personally, so I didn't *leave a message*   .

2 If I give you my phone, you can _____ through my vacation photos.

3 We turned off our phones at the start of the movie to make sure they didn't _____.

4 We were _____ when the train I was on went into a tunnel.

5 I need to choose another _____ because I never hear the one I have.

6 I couldn't talk to my bank because the phone was _____.

7 When you call big companies, they often _____ you _____ for a long time.

8 John isn't answering his phone, so I'll have to _____ later.

9 Did you listen to your _____ last night? I left you a message.

10 I usually _____ when companies call me to try to sell me something.

11 I don't have to _____ my friends' numbers because they're all in my contacts.

12 Can you _____ your brother and tell him we're going to be late?

2 GRAMMAR obligation and prohibition

a Read the article. If both forms are correct, check (✔) the
   sentence. If only one form is correct, (circle) the correct form.

What you need to know before you visit
NEW YORK

1 You *have to / must* have a visa to enter the US. ✔

2 You (*must not*) */ don't have to* drive on the left!
   Here we drive on the right! ☐

3 You *must not / don't have to* pay to visit most museums
   and art galleries. Entrance is usually free. ☐

4 You *have to / must* visit the Statue of Liberty. It's very impressive. ☐

5 You *must not / don't have to* smoke in any public building.
   It is prohibited by law. ☐

6 You *have to / must* wear a seat belt at all times in a car. ☐

7 You *must not / don't have to* go everywhere by subway.
   You can take the bus. ☐

8 You *must / have to* answer some questions when you go
   through immigration. ☐

b Complete the sentences with *must*, *must not*, *should*, or *shouldn't*.

1 Adam *must*_____ graduate from high school or he won't be able to go to college.
2 I think you _____ buy the blue dress, not the red one. It suits you better.
3 You _____ take phones into the exam room.
4 You _____ eat so much junk food. It isn't good for you.
5 You _____ be quiet when you're in the library.
6 Who do you think we _____ invite to the party?
7 I know I _____ go out tonight, but I really want to go to the concert.
8 I _____ forget to call my sister back. She left me a message this morning.

c Correct any mistakes in the highlighted phrases. Check (✔) the correct sentences.

1 You must not read text messages when you're talking to somebody.
   You shouldn't read text messages ▢
2 Do you have to wear a suit and tie at work? ✔
3 I must go to work by bus yesterday. My car was being repaired. ▢
   _____
4 You don't look well. You should go home. ▢
   _____
5 You don't have to park here. It says "no parking." ▢
   _____
6 My father is a nurse and he often should work nights. ▢
   _____
7 In the future, perhaps everyone will have to speak English and Chinese. ▢
   _____
8 I must not cook last night because we went out for dinner. ▢
   _____

d Write a sentence about an obligation in each of the places. Use *must*, *have to*, *should*, and *ought to*.

1 an airport
   You should arrive two hours before
   the flight leaves.
2 a movie theater
   _____
   _____
3 a soccer stadium
   _____
   _____
4 a library
   _____
   _____
5 a museum
   _____
   _____
6 a swimming pool
   _____
   _____

3 PRONUNCIATION
silent consonants

a Cross out the silent consonants in the words.

1 listen
2 shouldn't
3 lights
4 hour
5 exhausted
6 debt
7 mortgage
8 foreign
9 wrong
10 island

b ◖) 4.1 Listen and check. Then listen again and repeat the words.

Go online for more practice

4B Yes, I can!

Failure is not falling down. Failure is
falling down and not getting up again.
Richard Nixon, former US President

G ability and possibility: *can, could, be able to,* reflexive pronouns | **V** *-ed / -ing* adjectives | **P** sentence stress

1 GRAMMAR ability and possibility, reflexive pronouns

a Read the sentences. If both forms are correct, check (✔) the sentence. If only one form is correct, (circle) the correct form.

1 She *can / is able to* swim really well because she used to live by the ocean. ✔

2 You need to *can /* (*be able to*) drive to live in the country.

3 Luke *could / was able to* read when he was only three years old.

4 If it doesn't rain tomorrow, *we can / we'll be able to* go for a long walk.

5 Sorry, I've been so busy that I *haven't could / haven't been able to* call until now.

6 If Mai-ting had a less demanding job, she *could / would be able to* enjoy life more.

7 I've never *could / been able to* dance well, but I'd love to learn.

8 We're really sorry we *couldn't / weren't able to* come to your wedding.

9 I *used to can / used to be able to* speak a little Arabic, but I've forgotten most of it now.

10 *Can you / Will you be able to* pick me up at the train station when I arrive?

11 To work for this company, you *must can / must be able to* speak at least three languages.

12 I hate *not can / not being able to* communicate with the local people when I'm traveling.

b Read Tyler Ruiz's résumé. Then complete the sentences with the correct form of *can, could,* or *be able to*.

1 Tyler *can* _____ sail.

2 He _____ speak a little Chinese when he started working in Hong Kong.

3 He _____ speak German.

4 He _____ design websites since 2004.

5 He _____ finish his PhD before he left the US.

6 He'd like _____ speak Russian.

7 He _____ speak a little Russian soon.

Name: Tyler Ruiz

Date of Birth: 09/22/1985

Education

- Degree in French with Marketing (2008)
- Master's in Business Administration (2011)
- Started PhD in Business (2014) – incomplete

Work Experience

- **2003–2005:** Trainer and Operator with Texas Instruments, London
- **2008–2014:** Assistant then Marketing Manager, Texas Instruments, Dallas, US
- **2014–present:** Managing Director, AHH Marketing Services Ltd., Hong Kong

Other Skills

- IT skills – advanced
- Course in web design 2004

Languages

- French (fluent)
- Chinese (basic) certificate 2013
- I hope to start Russian classes next January.

Hobbies and Interests

- Watersports, especially sailing and windsurfing

c Match the sentence halves.

1 Thanks for inviting me yesterday. I really enjoyed __c__
2 She got the job because she'd prepared ____
3 Have a great time, you two! I'm sure you'll enjoy ____
4 My new printer is much better than my old one. It even turns ____
5 We really wanted to watch the sunrise, so we kept ____
6 He fell down the stairs, but luckily he didn't hurt ____
7 They've been saving to buy ____

a himself badly.
b ourselves awake by listening to music.
c myself at the concert.
d itself off when it isn't being used.
e yourselves at the party.
f themselves a house since they got married.
g herself well for the interview.

2 PRONUNCIATION sentence stress

a ◑ 4.2 Listen and complete the sentences.

1 She can _sing_ very _well_.
2 I've _____ been _____ to _____.
3 Can you _____ the _____?
4 You _____ be _____ to _____.
5 He _____ been _____ to _____ to _____ _____.
6 We _____ the _____.

b ◑ 4.2 Listen again and repeat the sentences. Copy the rhythm.

3 VOCABULARY -ed / -ing adjectives

a Complete the sentences with the correct adjective in **bold**.

1 **amazed / amazing**
Venice is an _amazing_ city. You really must go there one day.

2 **embarrassed / embarrassing**
I felt very _____ when I realized my mistake.

3 **frightened / frightening**
He's _____ of dogs. He can't go anywhere near them.

4 **excited / exciting**
The final half of the game was really _____.

5 **bored / boring**
I enjoyed the book, but the movie was a little _____.

6 **annoyed / annoying**
I can't stand this quiz show. The host is really _____.

7 **depressed / depressing**
I'm fed up with this terrible weather – it's so _____.

8 **disappointed / disappointing**
Max was very _____ when he wasn't chosen for the job.

9 **tired / tiring**
Everyone was _____ after the walk, so nobody felt like going out in the evening.

10 **frustrated / frustrating**
I got very _____ when I couldn't log onto my bank's website.

b Complete the sentences with the *-ed* or *-ing* form of the verbs from the list.

amaze ~~annoy~~ bore depress disappoint
embarrass excite frighten frustrate tire

1 I'm really *annoyed* with my brother – it makes me so angry when he forgets my birthday!
2 My sister can't swim. She's _____ of the water.
3 Looking after small children can be very _____. They have a lot of energy.
4 I was very _____ when my phone rang during the meeting. I could feel my face getting red.
5 His class grades were very _____. He failed every subject.
6 I'm really _____ about going to Australia. It's the first time I've been abroad!
7 This show is really _____. Can we watch something more interesting?
8 I always feel _____ at the end of a vacation. Sometimes I'm unhappy for days!
9 She tried for a long time to get back onto the surfboard, but in the end she got _____ and gave up.
10 We took lots of photos because the view was so _____.

c Write true sentences about you using the words in **bold**.

1 **annoying**
My little brother is sometimes very annoying.

2 **bored**

3 **amazing**

4 **exciting**

5 **frightened**

6 **disappointed**

7 **frustrating**

8 **embarrassed**

Go online for more practice   Go online to check your progress

5A Sporting superstitions

Just play. Have fun. Enjoy the game.
Michael Jordan, US basketball player

| **G** past tenses: simple, continuous, perfect | **V** sports | **P** /ɔr/ and /ɜr/ |

1 VOCABULARY sports

a Read the definitions. Then write the words.

1 a large group of people who are watching a sporting event
cr<u>owd</u>

2 people who are very enthusiastic about a sport
f_____

3 an official who makes sure that players obey the rules in, e.g., soccer, basketball, ice hockey, etc.
r_____

4 a group of people who play a sport or game together against another group
t_____

5 an official who makes sure that players obey the rules, e.g., in baseball
u_____

6 people who play a game or sport
pl_____

7 a large structure, usually with no roof, where people can sit and watch sports
st_____

8 an area with seats around it where public entertainment such as sports events are held
a_____

9 the person who is the leader of a team
c_____

10 a person who trains people to compete in certain sports
c_____

11 people who are watching a sports event
sp_____

b Label the photos with a word from the list.

course   court   field   ~~pool~~   slope   track

1 swimming *pool*_____

2 tennis _____

3 golf _____

5 soccer _____

5 ski _____

6 running _____

c Complete the sentences with the simple past form of the verbs from the list.

| beat do get injured get in shape go |
| kick lose score tie throw train win |

1 My wife _did_____ yoga five times a week when she was younger.
2 The team _____ hard every day before the tournament.
3 The Moroccan runner _____ the race. He got the gold medal.
4 I _____ by riding my bike to work every day. Now I'm much healthier than I used to be.
5 Mexico and Spain _____ their game 2–2.
6 I didn't play well in the semi-final. I _____ 2–6, 1–6.
7 Marc _____ the ball to his brother, but he dropped it.
8 Brazil _____ the US 5–0 in the final. They had a much stronger team.
9 The Argentinian striker _____ four goals in the last game.
10 Our best player _____ in the second half and was taken to see the team's doctor.
11 We _____ swimming every day when we were on vacation.
12 Everyone laughed when I _____ the ball and my shoe came off.

d Complete the phrasal verbs in the sentences with the words from the list.

| off out (x2) up |

1 You get in shape quickly if you work _out_____ every day.
2 That player is going to be sent _____ if he continues arguing with the referee.
3 We'll be knocked _____ of the tournament if we don't win our next game.
4 You can get injured if you don't warm _____ before you play a game.

2 PRONUNCIATION /ɔr/ and /ɜr/

a Circle the word with a different sound.

ɔr horse	1 cour**se** wor**k out** four war**m up**
ɜr bird	2 f**ir**st h**ur**t sp**or**t w**or**ld
ɔr horse	3 d**oor** sh**or**ts sc**or**e sl**o**pe
ɜr bird	4 c**our**t s**er**ve c**ir**cuit w**or**se

b ◑5.1 Listen and check. Then listen again and repeat the words.

3 GRAMMAR past tenses

a Circle a, b, or c.

1 She ____ the gold medal at the last Olympic Games.
   a won **b** was winning **c** had won
2 I ____ breakfast when I heard the news.
   a had **b** was having **c** had had
3 I wanted to go for a swim, but I ____ a towel.
   a didn't bring **b** wasn't bringing **c** hadn't brought
4 Our guests arrived while we ____ the basketball game on TV.
   a watched **b** were watching **c** had watched
5 We ____ any goals in our last game.
   a didn't score **b** weren't scoring **c** hadn't scored
6 As soon as the movie started, I realized that I ____ it before.
   a saw **b** was seeing **c** had seen
7 I ____ ice hockey and tennis when I was in school.
   a played **b** was playing **c** had played
8 It was late and people ____ to get home before it got dark.
   a hurried **b** were hurrying **c** had hurried
9 We were exhausted when we eventually got home – we ____ a very busy day.
   a had **b** were having **c** had had
10 Sorry. I ____ when you called, so I couldn't answer.
   a drove **b** was driving **c** had driven

b Complete the sentences with the correct form of the verbs in parentheses. Use the simple past, past continuous, or past perfect.

1 When we *arrived* _____ (arrive), everyone else *had finished* _____ (finish) their lunch and they *were sitting* _____ (sit) on the patio having coffee.

2 They _____ (drive) to the airport when they suddenly _____ (remember) that they _____ (not lock) the back door.

3 I _____ (not recognize) many people at my school reunion because everyone _____ (change) a lot in the last 20 years.

4 My sister _____ (wait) to go out for dinner yesterday when her boyfriend _____ (call) her to say that he _____ (not can) come because his car _____ (break down).

5 Manchester City _____ (beat) Manchester United yesterday. United _____ (win) 1–0 in the first half, but City _____ (score) two goals in the second half.

6 He _____ (run) to the train station, but the nine o'clock train _____ (already / leave). The train station was empty except for two people who _____ (wait) for the next train.

c Complete the text with the correct form of the verbs in parentheses.

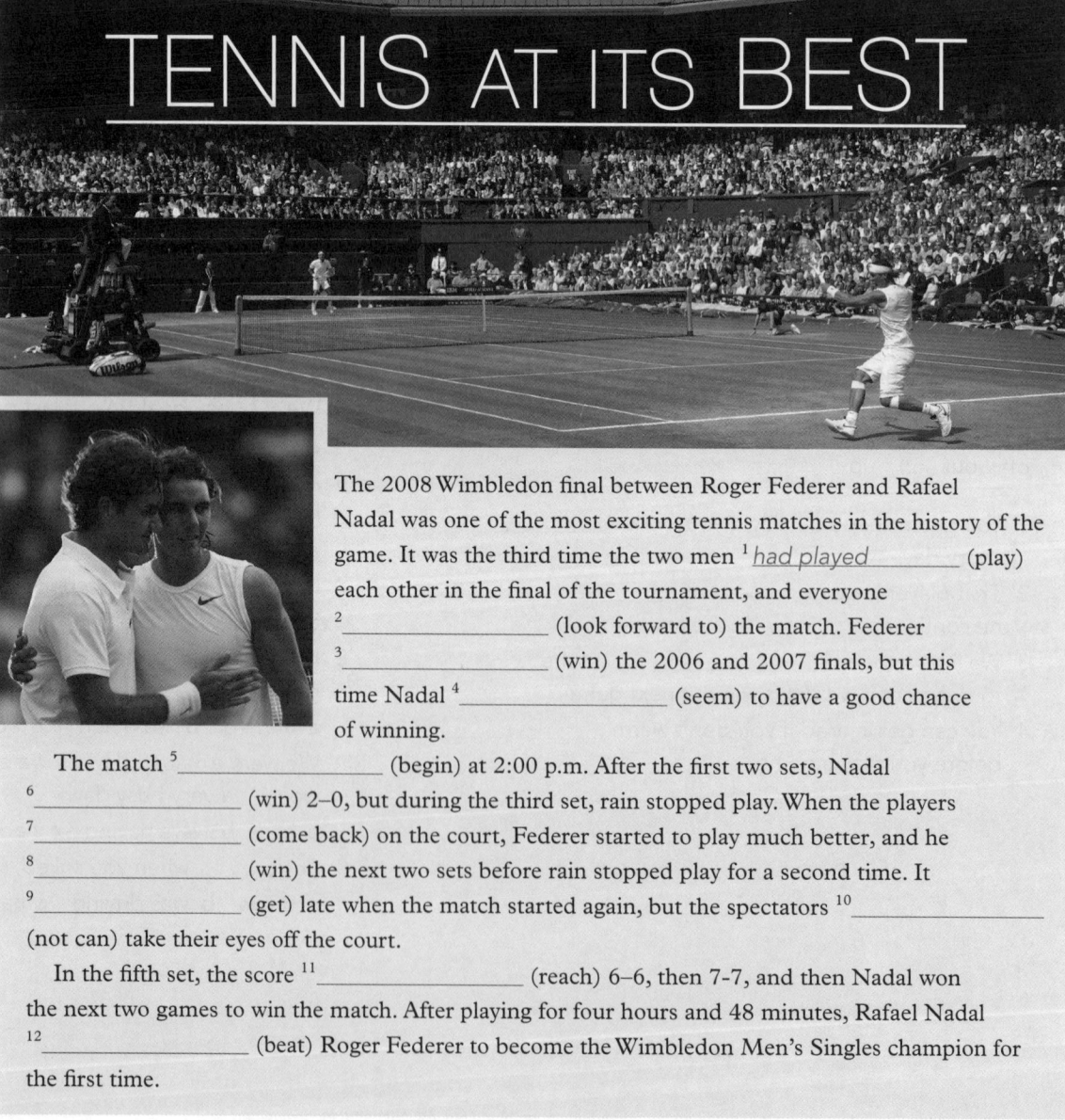

TENNIS AT ITS BEST

The 2008 Wimbledon final between Roger Federer and Rafael Nadal was one of the most exciting tennis matches in the history of the game. It was the third time the two men [1] *had played* _____ (play) each other in the final of the tournament, and everyone [2] _____ (look forward to) the match. Federer [3] _____ (win) the 2006 and 2007 finals, but this time Nadal [4] _____ (seem) to have a good chance of winning.

The match [5] _____ (begin) at 2:00 p.m. After the first two sets, Nadal [6] _____ (win) 2–0, but during the third set, rain stopped play. When the players [7] _____ (come back) on the court, Federer started to play much better, and he [8] _____ (win) the next two sets before rain stopped play for a second time. It [9] _____ (get) late when the match started again, but the spectators [10] _____ (not can) take their eyes off the court.

In the fifth set, the score [11] _____ (reach) 6–6, then 7-7, and then Nadal won the next two games to win the match. After playing for four hours and 48 minutes, Rafael Nadal [12] _____ (beat) Roger Federer to become the Wimbledon Men's Singles champion for the first time.

◯ **Go online** for more practice

Love is like war – easy to begin, but hard to end.
Anonymous

G past and present habits and states   **V** relationships   **P** the letter *s, used to*

1 GRAMMAR past and present habits and states

a Circle the correct words.

1 I *used to see / usually see* my friends two or three times a week. We often go to the movies.
2 Matt *used to play / usually plays* basketball, but he doesn't anymore.
3 We *didn't use to go / don't usually go* away on vacation because we can't afford it.
4 Jordan *used to wear / usually wears* makeup when she goes out.
5 *Did you use to have / Do you usually have* a lot of friends when you were at school?
6 We *stayed / usually stay* in the same cottage every summer when I was a child.
7 I *never used to watch / don't usually watch* much TV, but now I'm addicted to Netflix.
8 I *went skiing / used to go skiing* with some friends last weekend.

b Correct any mistakes in the highlighted phrases. Check (✔) the correct sentences.

1 Where did you used to live before you moved here?
   did you use to live
2 Jerry used to have a beard, but he shaved it off.   ✔

3 I usually go to the gym after work.

4 My wife doesn't use to wear high heels. She doesn't like them.

5 Did you use to have long hair when you were younger?

6 I use to walk to work. My office is only ten minutes from my house.

7 Carol never used to be very friendly, but now she always says hello to me.

8 Do you use to get up late on Sundays?

9 I used to go to Paris once with my parents when I was little.

10 We stayed in an expensive hotel when we were in Las Vegas.

c Complete the sentences with *usually*, or the correct form of *used to*, and the verbs in parentheses.

1 Naomi *used to wear* glasses, but now she has contact lenses. (wear)
2 My uncle and aunt _____ me a present on my birthday, but this year they forgot! (give)
3 I _____ my mom on Sundays. We talk for about half an hour. (call)
4 I _____ to French classes, but I stopped last month because I'm too busy now. (go)
5 We never _____, but now we go to a restaurant at least once a week. (eat out)
6 I _____ late, but today I need to finish this report before I go home. (not work)
7 My sister _____ very shy, but now she's much more confident. (be)
8 My boyfriend _____ animals, but now he has a dog. (not like)

2 PRONUNCIATION the letter s, used to

a 🔊 5.2 Listen and (circle) the word with a different sound.

![snake] 1 **s**nake	![zebra] 2 **z**ebra	![shower] 3 **sh**ower	![television] 4 televi**s**ion
see	eyes	ti**ss**ue	usually
(friends)	easy	please	pleasure
most	especially	sure	decision
social	nowadays	sugar	music

b 🔊 5.2 Listen again and repeat the words.

c 🔊 5.3 Listen and repeat. Copy the rhythm.

1 **Where** did you **use** to **live**?
2 Did you **use** to **wear glasses**?
3 They **used** to **have** a lot of **money**.
4 He **used** to **go** to my **school**.
5 We **used** to **work together**.
6 You **used** to **have long hair**.
7 We **didn't use** to **get along**.
8 I **didn't use** to **like** it.

3 VOCABULARY relationships

a Complete the sentences with the people from the list.

classmates   close friend   colleague
couple   ex   fiancé   ~~partner~~   roommate

1 Jack's divorced, but he has a new _partner_ named Kerry.
2 This is Koji, my _____. We're getting married next year.
3 Marisol is a very _____. I tell her everything.
4 That girl over there is my _____. We went out together for two years.
5 Tony and I were _____ in high school.
6 I went to the conference with a _____ from work.
7 Zoe is a great _____. She's good company, and she's very neat.
8 Emilio and Megan are a very nice _____. We've known them since college.

b Read about two relationships. Complete the phrases with a word from the list.

became   common   got   in   liked   married
~~met~~   out   proposed   to   together   touch   up

1 They _met_ at a party.
2 She _____ him.
3 She got _____ touch.
4 They went _____ together.
5 They didn't have a lot in _____.
6 They broke _____.
7 They lost _____.

8 They got _____ know each other.
9 They _____ along.
10 They _____ friends.
11 They were _____.
12 He _____ to her.
13 They got _____.

c Complete the text with the highlighted words and phrases from **b**. Use the simple past form of the verbs.

File   Edit   Window   Help

My photos

Work

Music

Website

IMG_1304

Anna [1] *met* _____ Luke when she started work. She [2] _____ immediately because he seemed like a really nice person. The two sat next to each other in the office, so they [3] _____ each other very quickly. They soon [4] _____, and they discovered that they [5] _____ because they were both sports fans. They [6] _____ a few times after work, and they fell in love.

They [7] _____ for a year, but they argued a lot, and in the end they [8] _____. After that, Anna got a new job in a different town and so they [9] _____. Ten years later, they [10] _____ again on Facebook. They were both still single, and Luke had changed jobs, too. They decided to try again, and this time they [11] _____ better than before, maybe because they weren't working together. After six months, Luke [12] _____ Anna, and she accepted. They [13] _____ last spring. A lot of their old colleagues from work came to the wedding!

d Complete the sentences with abstract nouns formed from the words from the list.

friend   leader   member   partner   ~~relation~~

1 My dad and I are very close. We have an excellent *relationship* _____.
2 My _____ with Debbie goes back to when we were in high school together. We've known each other for years!
3 I like the look of the new gym in my town, so I'm going to apply for a _____.
4 Karen was promoted to manager because of her _____ skills.
5 The two brothers have gone into _____ together, and they've opened a restaurant by the river.

Go online for more practice   Go online to check your progress

37

1 PERMISSION AND REQUESTS

a Re-order the words to make phrases for permission and requests.

1 jacket / pass / you / can / my
Can you pass my jacket _____?

2 OK / window / I / is / open / if / a / it
_____?

3 mind / that / would / repeating / you
_____?

4 you / of / take / me / a / could / photo
_____?

5 you / if / here / mind / sit / do / I
_____?

6 you / do / could / you / bag / carry / think / my
_____?

b Circle the best response to the questions from **a**.

1 *Yes, I can. / Sure.*
2 *No problem. / Yes, it is.*
3 *No, I wouldn't. / Not at all.*
4 *No problem. / Yes, I could.*
5 *Of course not. / No, I don't.*
6 *Yes, I could. / Sure.*

c Complete the requests with the correct form of a verb from the list.

do   join   meet   pass   take   visit

1 Could you *do* _____ me a big favor?
2 Is it OK if we _____ my parents this weekend?
3 Would you mind _____ me at the airport?
4 Do you mind if I _____ you?
5 Can you _____ the salt?
6 Do you think you could _____ me to the train station?

d Match the requests from **c** to responses a–f.

a _4_ Of course not. Take a seat.
b ____ Sure. Here it is.
c ____ Yes, of course. What time's your train?
d ____ It depends on what it is!
e ____ Not at all. When do you land?
f ____ Sure. Which day would be best?

2 SOCIAL ENGLISH

a Complete the highlighted phrases in the conversations with a word from the list.

come   days   mind   see   talk   way

1 A Hello, Richie. You're here at last!
  B Hi, Andy. It's great to see _____ you, mate.

2 A Come and sit down, Amelia. It's been a long time.
  B I know. We've got a lot to _____ about.

3 A How _____ you're so late?
  B Sorry, I missed the bus.

4 A This is nice. You and me having dinner together.
  B Yeah. Just like the old _____.

5 A Let's go out tonight.
  B I'd rather stay in, if you don't _____.

6 A Let's walk to the station.
  B No _____, man! Let's get a taxi!

b Complete the conversation with the highlighted phrases from **a**.

Jay Dan! ¹*It's great to see you.* _____
Dan You too, Jay. It's been years.
Jay ² _____
Dan My flight was delayed, and then I had to wait a long time for a taxi.
Jay Well, you're here now. Do you want to go to the hotel to rest?
Dan ³ _____ I want to go out and see the city!
Jay Don't you want to unpack first?
Dan No, I can do that later. But I'll take a shower, ⁴ _____
Jay Sure. Go ahead.
Dan This is great. You and me getting ready to go out.
Jay Yeah. ⁵ _____

***

Dan OK, I'm ready. Let's go. ⁶ _____
Jay That's true. So much has happened since we last saw each other.

Go online to practice the Practical English phrases

1 GRAMMAR

Complete the second sentence so that it has a similar meaning to the first sentence. Write three words. Contractions are two words, e.g., *isn't*.

1 I met my partner six years ago.
I've known my partner _____.

2 I'll carry that suitcase for you.
_____ that suitcase for you?

3 Jacob started studying at 9:00 a.m., and he's still studying now.
Jacob _____ since 9:00 a.m.

4 Playing soccer is prohibited in the pedestrian zone.
You _____ soccer in the pedestrian zone.

5 I can't go to your party next Friday.
I won't _____ go to your party next Friday.

6 My sister cried a lot when she was a child.
As a child, my sister _____ a lot.

2 VOCABULARY

Circle the word that is different.

1 boiled   canned   roasted   steamed
2 selfish   stubborn   bossy   reliable
3 tax   voicemail   budget   loan
4 scooter   road work   traffic light   crosswalk
5 call back   dial   hang up   propose
6 captain   stadium   coach   referee

3 PRONUNCIATION

Circle the word with a different sound.

🐂 bull	1	c**ou**ld f**oo**d g**oo**d s**u**gar
👢 boot	2	l**o**se p**oo**l c**oo**k h**u**ge
💻 computer	3	pr**o**pose m**o**rtgage c**o**mpetitive av**o**cado
🐴 horse	4	c**ou**rse f**o**rk sc**o**re w**o**rld
🐦 bird	5	h**u**rt sp**o**rt **ea**rn w**o**rse

4 GRAMMAR & VOCABULARY

Complete the article. Write one word in each space.

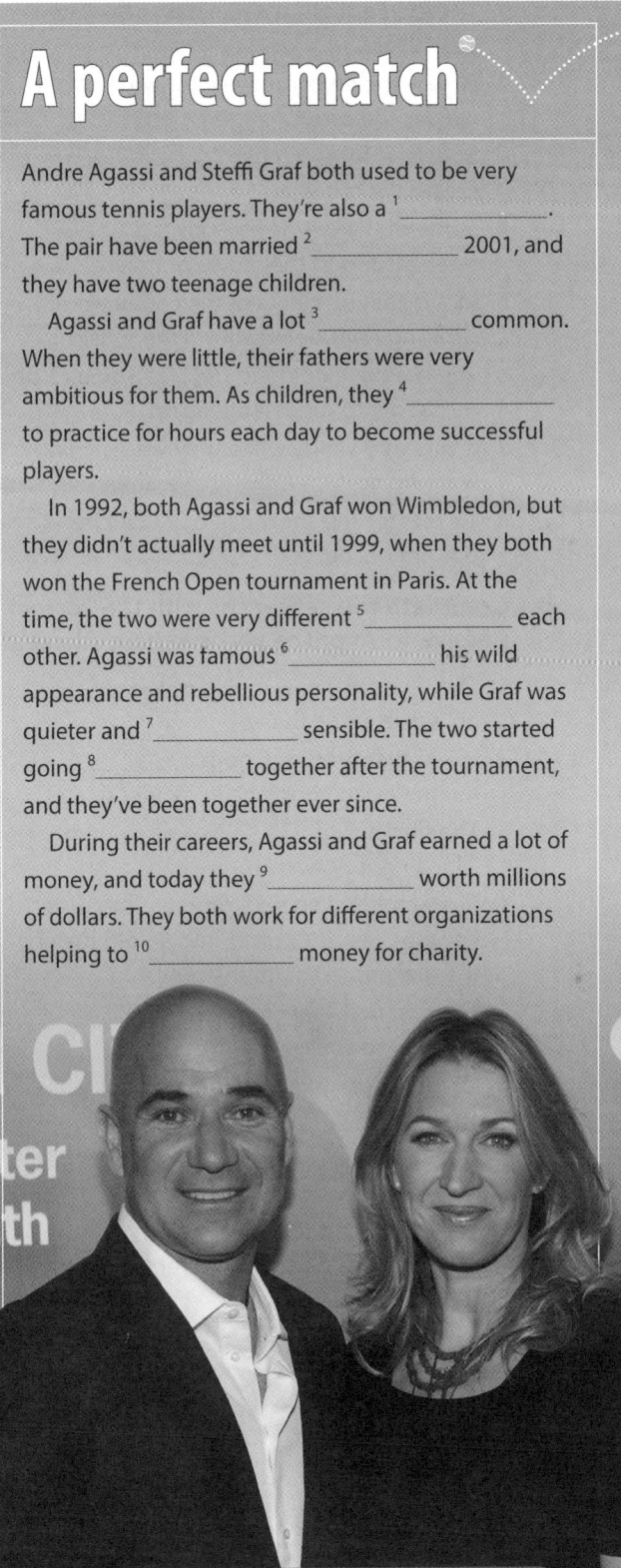

A perfect match

Andre Agassi and Steffi Graf both used to be very famous tennis players. They're also a [1]_____. The pair have been married [2]_____ 2001, and they have two teenage children.

Agassi and Graf have a lot [3]_____ common. When they were little, their fathers were very ambitious for them. As children, they [4]_____ to practice for hours each day to become successful players.

In 1992, both Agassi and Graf won Wimbledon, but they didn't actually meet until 1999, when they both won the French Open tournament in Paris. At the time, the two were very different [5]_____ each other. Agassi was famous [6]_____ his wild appearance and rebellious personality, while Graf was quieter and [7]_____ sensible. The two started going [8]_____ together after the tournament, and they've been together ever since.

During their careers, Agassi and Graf earned a lot of money, and today they [9]_____ worth millions of dollars. They both work for different organizations helping to [10]_____ money for charity.

✓ **Go online** to check your progress

> Film is one of three universal languages, the other two: mathematics and music.
> *Frank Capra, US movie director*

G passive (all tenses) **V** movies **P** regular and irregular past participles

1 GRAMMAR passive (all tenses)

a Circle the correct form, active or passive.

1 The movie *sets / is set* in New York City in the 1980s.
2 A well-known comedy writer *wrote / was written* the script.
3 Special effects *will use / will be used* to create the monster.
4 Some of the extras *have invited / have been invited* to the movie premiere.
5 Movie theaters all over the country *are showing / are being shown* the musical.
6 The drama *is going to dub / is going to be dubbed* into other languages.
7 It was very windy while they *were filming / were being filmed* the final scenes.
8 Tickets for the show *can buy / can be bought* online.

b Complete the sentences with the correct passive form of the verbs in parentheses.

1 The director's new movie *is based* on a true story. (base)
2 I read that Bradley Cooper _____ for an Oscar. I hope he wins! (nominate)
3 The final scene _____ in Africa right now. (film)
4 The actor looked very different because he _____ into an old man by the makeup artist. (transform)
5 The first *Star Wars* movies _____ by George Lucas. (direct)
6 One of the workers fell off a ladder while the set _____. (build)
7 The sequel _____ next year. (release)
8 The scene had to _____ several times before the director was satisfied. (shoot)

c Read the article. Circle a, b, or c.

STEVEN SPIELBERG
Four decades of movie history

Steven Spielberg [1]____ movies for over 40 years. The movie that made him famous around the world was *Jaws*, which [2]____ in 1975. *Jaws* [3]____ the story of a vacation resort where swimmers [4]____ by a huge great white shark. Spielberg had many problems with the mechanical sharks while the movie [5]____, but he managed to finish it in the end. *Jaws* was extremely successful, and it [6]____ three Academy Awards. Since then, Spielberg [7]____ many movies that have since become classics, including *Close Encounters of the Third Kind, E.T.,* and *Jurassic Park*. He [8]____ for an Oscar seven times and has won the award for Best Director twice: for *Schindler's List* and *Saving Private Ryan*. Today, Spielberg [9]____ to be one of the most popular directors and producers in movie history. Now in his seventies, he's still making movies, and it seems unlikely that he [10]____ any time soon.

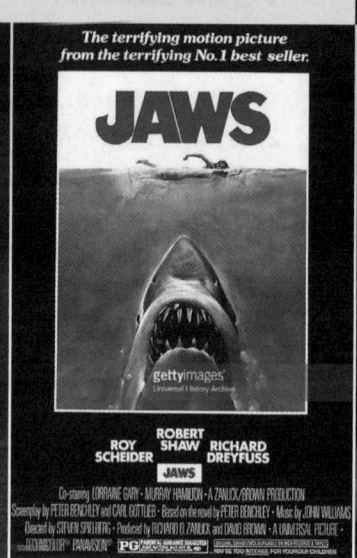

The terrifying motion picture from the terrifying No.1 best seller. **JAWS**

1 **a** has been making **b** has been made **c** is made
2 **a** is released **b** released **c** was released
3 **a** is told **b** tells **c** was told
4 **a** are being attacked **b** are attacking **c** attack
5 **a** was shot **b** shoot **c** was being shot
6 **a** was won **b** won **c** was being won
7 **a** has been directed **b** has directed **c** was directed
8 **a** nominated **b** has nominated **c** has been nominated
9 **a** considers **b** is considered **c** has been considered
10 **a** will retire **b** will be retired **c** is retired

2 PRONUNCIATION regular and irregular past participles

a Look at the past participles. Which sounds do the letters in **bold** have? Write the words from the list in the correct column in the chart.

said sh**o**t taken **taugh**t t**o**ld us**ed** wait**ed** ~~watch**ed**~~ w**o**n wri**tt**en

t tie	1 finish**ed** look**ed** releas**ed** *watched*
d dog	2 film**ed** play**ed** own**ed**
/ɪd/ /ɪd/	3 add**ed** direct**ed** repeat**ed**
fish	4 b**ui**lt g**i**ven h**i**t
a clock	5 forg**o**tten g**o**ne g**o**tten
ɔ saw	6 br**ough**t dr**aw**n f**a**llen
ɜ egg	7 f**e**lt l**e**ft m**ea**nt
ʌ up	8 d**o**ne dr**u**nk r**u**n
eɪ train	9 b**a**sed m**a**de p**ai**d
oʊ phone	10 ch**o**sen fl**ow**n st**o**len

b 🔊 6.1 Listen and check. Then listen again and repeat the groups of words.

3 VOCABULARY movies

a Match the words from the list to definitions 1–12.

action movie   animated movie   ~~comedy~~
drama   historical movie   horror movie
musical   rom-com   science fiction movie
thriller   war movie   western

1 an amusing movie that has a happy ending
   comedy

2 a movie that has a lot of exciting events, e.g., fights and car chases
   _____

3 a movie about imaginary events in the future
   _____

4 a movie with a serious story
   _____

5 a movie where the cast sings and dances
   _____

6 a movie with an exciting story, often about a crime
   _____

7 a movie based on real events in the past
   _____

8 a scary movie
   _____

9 a movie about soldiers fighting battles
   _____

10 a movie about life in the past in the US
   _____

11 a movie that is made with pictures that appear to move
   _____

12 a funny movie about love
   _____

b Complete the sentences.

1 The st*ar*_____ of the movie was a famous American actress.

2 I didn't understand the movie because the pl_____ was very complicated.

3 The actor wanted to play the part as soon as he had read the sc_____.

4 Some of the a_____ was crying at the end of the movie.

5 Most critics have given the movie an excellent r_____.

6 They only had to shoot the sc_____ once.

7 It's a French movie, but with English s_____.

8 You'll have to wait for the s_____ to find out what happens next.

9 My favorite s_____ is the music from *Guardians of the Galaxy*.

10 The best thing about the movie was the sp_____ e_____. They were very realistic.

11 The director is looking for e_____ to act in the crowd scenes.

12 The c_____ was a mixture of British and American actors.

13 *The Times* movie cr_____ didn't like the movie at all.

14 The two actors first met on the s_____ of the movie *La La Land*.

15 I've seen the tr_____, and it looks like a really interesting movie.

c Complete the text with the phrases from the list.

is based on   ~~was directed by~~   was dubbed into
plays the part of   is set in   was shot

THE REVENANT

The Revenant is a 2015 American western. It ¹*was directed by* Mexican movie director Alejandro G. Iñárritu. The movie ²_____ the northwestern part of the US. It ³_____ a novel about the experiences of Hugh Glass, a man who lived in the area in the early 1800s. *The Revenant* ⁴_____ on location in Canada, the US, and Argentina. Leonardo DiCaprio ⁵_____ Hugh Glass and won an Academy Award for his performance. *The Revenant* was made in English, but it ⁶_____ other languages.

Go online for more practice

6B Every picture tells a story

G modals of deduction: *might, can't, must* **V** the body **P** diphthongs

1 GRAMMAR modals of deduction

a Circle the correct words.

1 That man *can't* / *must* be the new boss. Our new boss is a woman.

2 You *must* / *can't* be really tired. You've had a long trip.

3 I'm not sure what book to buy Austin. He *might not* / *must not* like the same kind of things as me.

4 Paula *can't* / *could* be injured. She isn't running very well at all today. She's very slow.

5 Your neighbor *must* / *might not* have a good job. He has a very expensive car.

6 Luke and Molly *must* / *can't* have much money. They never go out.

b Complete the sentences with *must, might, might not,* or *can't*.

1 He lived in Argentina for five years, so he <u>must</u> speak good Spanish!

2 You _____ be very busy at work. You're always on Facebook!

3 I'm not sure, but the new assistant _____ be South Korean. Her last name is Cho.

4 Mark passed all his exams. His parents _____ be very proud.

5 **A** I think Mexico will win tonight.
   B You _____ be serious! They don't have a chance!

6 Lucy wasn't feeling well this afternoon, so she _____ come to the party tonight. She said she'd let us know later today.

7 I thought our neighbor was away on vacation, but she _____ be – I just saw her drive down the street.

8 It's very cold and cloudy this evening. I think it _____ snow.

c Rewrite the highlighted sentences. Use *might (not), can't,* or *must*.

1 They've been knocked out of the tournament. I'm sure they're disappointed.
   They <u>must be disappointed</u>.

2 Emily's late. It's possible that she has a meeting.
   She _____.

3 It's 8:30 and Tomo's still in bed. I'm sure he isn't going to work today.
   He _____.

4 Don't buy that sweater for Maya. It's possible that she won't like it.
   She _____.

5 We've only walked for 15 minutes. I'm sure you aren't tired already.
   You _____.

6 Shira's been studying all night. I'm sure she has an exam tomorrow.
   She _____.

7 We've been waiting a long time for the elevator. It's possible that it isn't working.
   It _____.

8 My brother isn't answering his phone. It's possible that he's driving home from work.
   He _____.

2 VOCABULARY the body

a Label the picture.

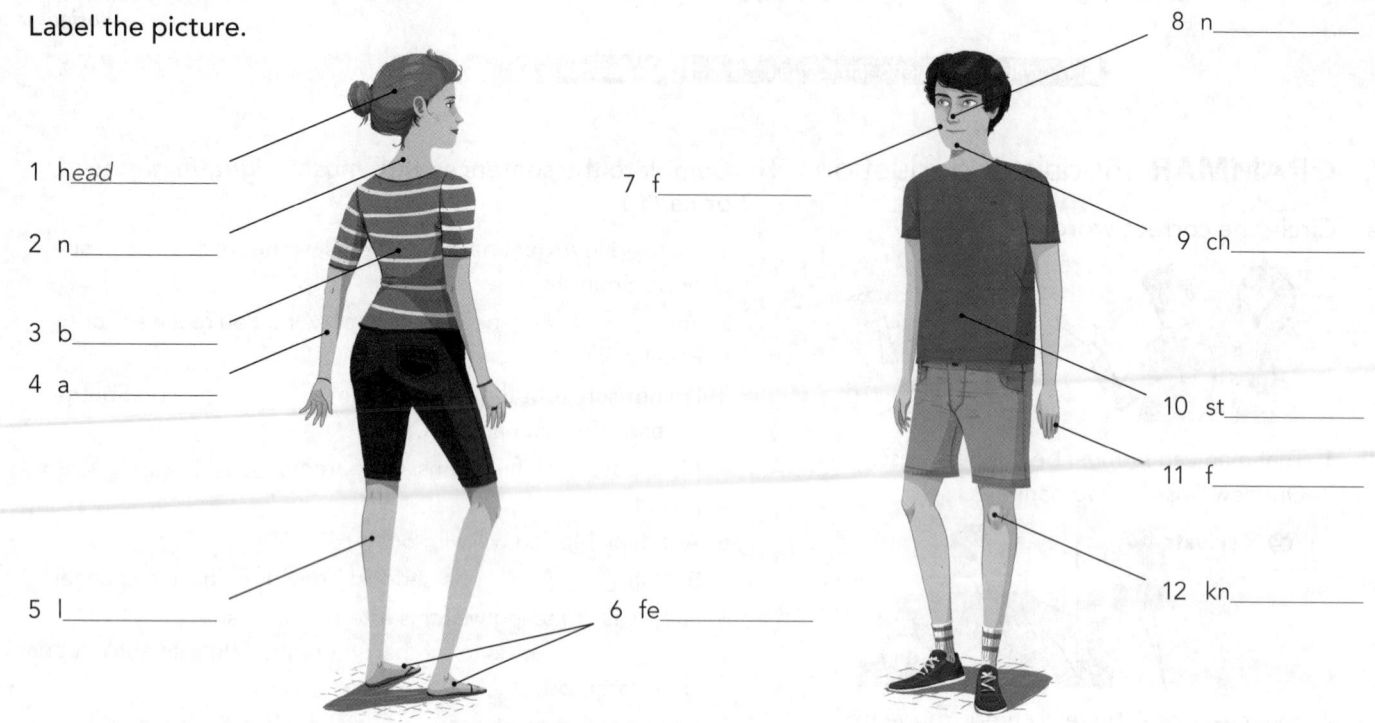

1 h_ead_____

2 n_____

3 b_____

4 a_____

5 l_____

6 fe_____

7 f_____

8 n_____

9 ch_____

10 st_____

11 f_____

12 kn_____

b Look at the pictures. Complete the puzzle to find the hidden part of the body.

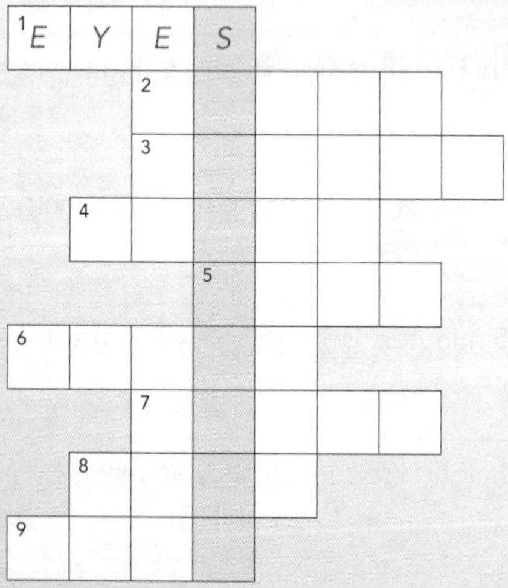

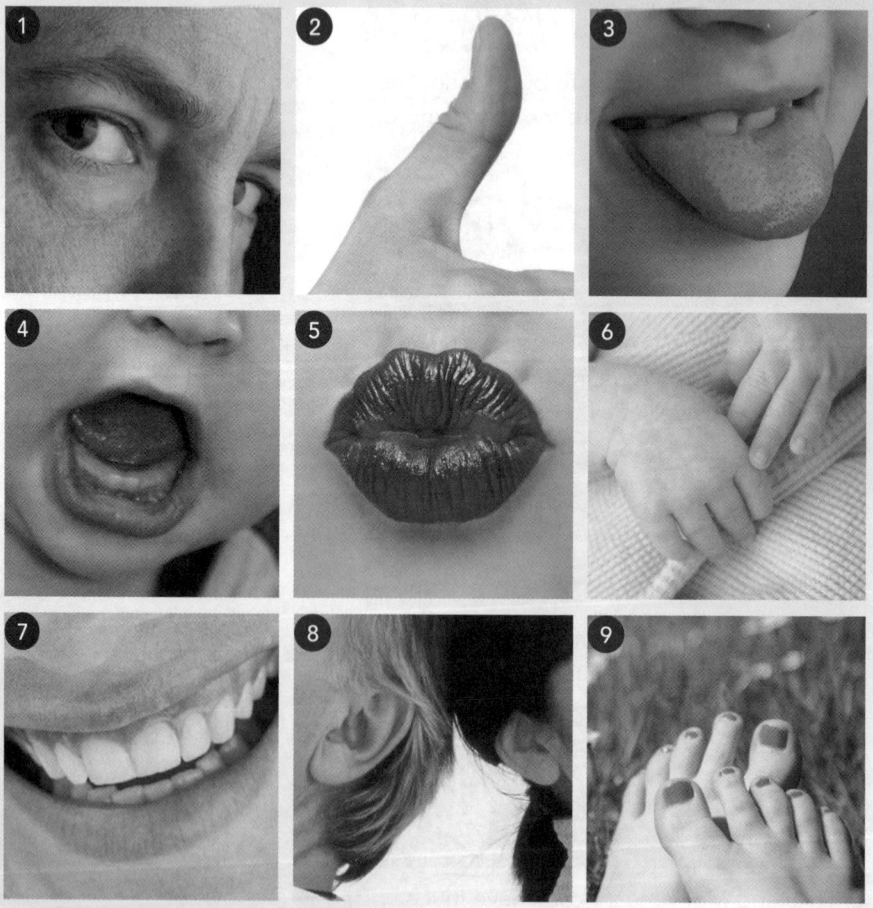

¹E	Y	E	S

c Complete the sentences with a verb from the list.

bite clap kick nod point smell
smile ~~stare~~ taste throw touch whistle

1 It's rude to _stare_ at people. It can make them feel uncomfortable.
2 You'll have to _____ the ball harder to score a goal.
3 Don't _____ that plant with your hand – it's poisonous.
4 If you're in another country and don't speak the language, you can _____ at the thing you want in a store or café.
5 I can _____ something burning. Did you turn off the oven?
6 My grandparents always look unhappy in photos because they never _____ at the camera.
7 He was too embarrassed to speak, but he was able to _____ his head to show he had understood.
8 Did the audience _____ much at the end of the concert?
9 Laila doesn't like dogs because she's afraid they'll _____ her.
10 I often _____ my favorite song when I'm in the shower.
11 Don't drop trash on the street. _____ it in the trash can.
12 Can you _____ the soup? I think it might need more salt.

d Complete the sentences with a part of the body.

1 You kick with your _foot_.
2 You point with your _____.
3 You smile with your _____.
4 You taste with your _____.
5 You nod with your _____.
6 You stare with your _____.
7 You smell with your _____.
8 You touch with your _____.
9 You whistle with your _____.
10 You bite with your _____.
11 You clap with your _____.

3 PRONUNCIATION diphthongs

a (Circle) the word with a different sound.

aɪ bike	1 bite smile h**eigh**t (w**eigh**t)	
eɪ train	2 f**a**ce gr**ea**t **eye**s t**a**ste	
oʊ phone	3 n**o**se t**o**ngue thr**ow** t**oe**s	
aʊ owl	4 s**ou**nd cr**ow**d m**ou**th sh**ou**lders	
ɔɪ boy	5 ch**oi**ce j**oy** t**ou**ch v**oi**ce	

b 🔊 6.2 Listen and check. Then listen again and repeat the words.

🔵 **Go online** for more practice   ✓ **Go online** to check your progress

One child, one teacher, one book, one pen can change the world.
Malala Yousafzai

G first conditional and future time clauses + *when, until,* etc. **V** education **P** the letter *u*

1 VOCABULARY education

a Complete the sentences. Order the letters to make school subjects.

1 *Physics* (siphycs) is the scientific study of natural forces such as light, sound, heat, electricity, pressure, etc.

2 _____ (ogphyrage) is the study of the world's surface, physical qualities, climate, countries, products, population, etc.

3 _____ (lobigyo) is the scientific study of living things.

4 _____ (teturelira) is the study of poetry, drama, and fiction.

5 _____ (trymische) is the scientific study of substances and what happens to them in different conditions.

6 _____ (rytohis) is the study of past events.

7 _____ _____ (fortionmain nogytechlo) is the study of computers for collecting, storing, and sending out information.

8 _____ (eticsmamath) is the study of numbers, quantities, or shapes.

b Match the words from the list to definitions 1–11.

In the US

college   elementary school   grade   high school
kindergarten   middle school   preschool
private school   public school   religious school
semesters

1 A school for children aged from about two to five
preschool

2 A school supported by US tax dollars
_____

3 A school for children aged from 11 to 13
_____

4 A school that parents have to pay for
_____

5 a school level with children of the same age
_____

6 A school where teachers may be priests or nuns
_____

7 A school for children aged from five to ten
_____

8 A place where students can study for a degree after they have finished high school
_____

9 A class to prepare children aged five for first grade
_____

10 A school for children aged 13 to 18
_____

11 A period of time that the school year is divided into
_____

c Complete the sentences.

In the UK

1 Very young children often go to n*ursery* sch*ool*.

2 Children start p_____ sch_____ when they are five.

3 Children go to s_____ sch_____ from the ages of 11 to 18.

4 The school year is divided into three t_____.

5 A school where children study, eat, and sleep is a b_____ sch_____.

6 School children are usually called p_____.

7 When they leave school, some students go to u_____ to continue their education.

d Complete the texts with the simple past form of the verbs from the list.

be punished   ~~be suspended~~   cheat   let   make
misbehave   (not) be allowed to

At my private high school, discipline was very strict. Students who behaved badly ¹*were suspended*, so very few students ²_____ in class. We ³_____ talk during class, and the teacher ⁴_____ us stand up every time another teacher came into the classroom. We had to wear a uniform, and we ⁵_____ if we wore something different. We had to study a lot, and nobody ⁶_____ on exams. In the final year, the teachers weren't as strict with us, and they ⁷_____ us leave school during the lunch break.

fail   pass   study   take

I was very nervous before my final exams in college. I ⁸_____ for several weeks, and I didn't go out at all. I ⁹_____ five exams, and I was very relieved when I had finished. In the end, I ¹⁰_____ all of them, but my friends weren't so lucky. They ¹¹_____ some of the exams, so they had to retake the classes.

2 PRONUNCIATION the letter *u*

a Circle the word with a different sound.

u boot	1 fr**ui**t	**lunch** sc**oo**ter tr**ue**
↑ **u**p	2 c**ou**ple m**u**ssels p**u**ll t**o**ngue
℧ b**u**ll	3 c**u**t f**u**ll p**u**sh p**u**t
/yu/ /yu/	4 f**u**ture m**u**scial t**u**na **u**niform

b 🔊 7.1 Listen and check. Then listen again and repeat the words.

3 GRAMMAR first conditional and future time clauses + *when*, *until*, etc.

a Match the sentence halves.

1 Will you buy a car _____e_____
2 Mike's parents will be furious _____
3 I'll have more time to help you _____
4 You'll have to go to a new school _____
5 He won't pass his exams _____
6 Nina won't go back to work _____
7 You'll need to buy the book _____
8 I'll stay at home _____

a unless he studies more.
b after I come back from my vacation.
c if he fails his exam again.
d before the classes start.
e ~~if you pass your driver's test?~~
f when your family moves to California.
g if I still don't feel well in the morning.
h until her daughter starts school.

b Complete the sentences with a word from the list. Use each word only once.

after   before   if   ~~unless~~   until   when

1 They won't be able to leave class _unless_ the teacher gives them permission.
2 They'll have to wear a uniform _____ they go to a private school.
3 I'll talk to my teachers _____ I choose the subjects I want to study next semester.
4 Emmi will be disappointed _____ she doesn't get good grades.
5 I'll have a long vacation _____ the semester finishes.
6 The teacher won't start class _____ all the students are quiet.

c Complete the sentences with the correct form of the verbs in parentheses. Use the simple present or future (*will / won't*).

1 I _'ll do_ my homework as soon as I _get_ home. (do, get)
2 We _____ late unless we _____. (be, hurry)
3 I _____ a shower before I _____. (take, go out)
4 The school bus _____ for you if you _____ on time. (not wait, not be)
5 If the teacher _____, we _____ the exam. (not come, not have)
6 James _____ home until he _____ a job. (not leave, find)
7 Alice _____ buy a car unless her parents _____ her the money. (not be able to, lend)
8 As soon as my boyfriend _____ his grades, he _____ me. (get, call)
9 She _____ kindergarten until she _____ five years old. (not start, be)
10 You _____ better if you _____ every day. (play, practice)

d Complete the sentences with your own ideas.

1 I'll charge my phone _when I get home tonight_____.
2 I'll go out tonight if _____.
3 I won't watch TV later unless _____.
4 I'll do my homework before _____.
5 I won't buy a (new) phone until _____.
6 I'll go to bed after _____.

Ⓝ **Go online** for more practice

1 GRAMMAR second conditional, choosing between conditionals

a Match the sentence halves.

1 If we had the time, __*d*__
2 I'd like my apartment more ____
3 You'd be able to find a job ____
4 If my sister didn't work so hard, ____
5 If we bought a bigger house with a yard, ____
6 If they could live anywhere they wanted to, ____
7 We'd get along better ____
8 I wouldn't want to live in New York City, ____

a she could spend more time with her children.
b they'd move to Hawaii.
c if you spoke better English.
d ~~we'd do the housework ourselves.~~
e if we didn't have to share an office.
f unless I earned a lot of money.
g if it was on the top floor.
h we'd be able to have a dog.

b Complete the sentences with the correct form of the verbs in parentheses. Use the second conditional.

1 If Tom *had* ____ more time, he*'d paint* ____ his room himself. (have, paint)
2 Lucy ____ happier if her roommate ____ the kitchen more often. (be, clean)
3 I ____ to work if I ____ a parking space. (not drive, not have)
4 ____ you ____ working if you ____ a lot of money? (continue, win)
5 I'm sure Antonia ____ better if she ____ so much coffee. (sleep, not drink)
6 My parents ____ me the money if I ____ to buy a new car. (lend, need)
7 I ____ surprised if it ____ tonight. (not be, snow)
8 If our house ____ so small, you ____ all stay the night. (not be, can)
9 ____ you ____ if you ____ your alarm? (wake up, not set)
10 If we ____ another bathroom, there ____ a line for the shower. (have, not be)

c Complete the sentences with the words in parentheses. Use the first or second conditional.

1 If they offer me the job, *I'll take it* ____. (I / take it)
2 If my car wasn't being repaired, *I'd give you a lift* ____. (I / give you a lift)
3 If I had Emily's number, ____. (I / call her)
4 You'll miss the train if ____. (you / not hurry up)
5 If I see John, ____. (I / tell him the news)
6 Rob wouldn't send you flowers if ____. (he / not love you)
7 If my mother didn't live on her own, ____. (she / be happier)
8 If it rains on Saturday, ____. (they / cancel the game)
9 You wouldn't spend so much money if ____. (you / not eat out every night).
10 Rita won't go to work tomorrow if ____. (she / not feel better)

2 PRONUNCIATION sentence stress, the letter *c*

a ◖) 7.2 Listen and complete the sentences.

1 If I *exercised* ____ more, I'd be in much *better shape* ____.
2 I'd ____ my own ____ if I had a ____.
3 Would you ____ a ____ if you ____?
4 If it were ____, I ____ the ____.
5 I ____ a ____ if I ____ in the ____.

b ◖) 7.2 Listen again and repeat the sentences. <u>Copy</u> the <u>rhy</u>thm.

c Say the pairs of words. Do the letters in **bold** have the same pronunciation or are they pronounced differently? Write **S** (same) or **D** (different).

1 **c**arpet   lo**c**ation   _S_
2 **c**abin   **c**eiling   _D_
3 **c**enter   **c**ozy   ____
4 spa**c**ious   spe**c**ial   ____
5 **c**ity   **c**enter   ____
6 **c**astle   musi**c**ian   ____
7 de**c**ide   entran**c**e   ____
8 firepla**c**e   bal**c**ony   ____

d 🔊 7.3 Listen and check. Then listen again and repeat the words.

3 VOCABULARY houses

a Complete the sentences with *in* or *on*.

1 We're looking for a house _in_ a suburb. We don't want to live in the city.
2 I'd love to live by the ocean, maybe ____ the west coast.
3 All the bedrooms are ____ the second floor.
4 Sara bought a beautiful cabin ____ the woods, where she can go hiking every day.
5 Chris lives ____ the outskirts of the city, so he has to commute to work in the city every day.
6 My grandparents live ____ a town north of New York City called Cold Spring.

b Complete the crossword.

DOWN ↓

1 the part of the building that covers the top part of it
3 the highest floor of a building
4
6 the space or room under the roof of a house
7
9

ACROSS →

2 a flat, hard area, especially outside a house or restaurant, where you can sit, eat, and enjoy the sun
5
7 a room or rooms in a building, partly or completely below the ground
8 one of the sides of a room or building joining the ceiling to the floor
10 the floor of a building that is at street level
11
12

c Complete the ads. Circle a, b, or c.

JUST ADDED

FOR SALE

This [1]____ apartment is on the top floor of a building with magnificent views of the Charles River. All the rooms are very [2]____. It has three bedrooms, a bathroom, and a large [3]____ kitchen. The living room has a [4]____ floor, and there are carpets in all the bedrooms.

1 **a** modern **b** recent **c** young
2 **a** clear **b** light **c** lit
3 **a** big **b** spacious **c** tiny
4 **a** board **b** rug **c** wood

SUBURB LOCATION

FOR SALE

This 1980s cabin is situated in a quiet suburb. It has a kitchen, bathroom, living room, and two small but [5]____ bedrooms. All the rooms have low [6]____, and the walls are made [7]____ logs. There is a large [8]____ in the living room, but the cabin also has central heat.

5 **a** cozy **b** safe **c** soft
6 **a** ceilings **b** roofs **c** walls
7 **a** by **b** in **c** of
8 **a** roof **b** fireplace **c** patio

3 BEDROOMS

FOR SALE

This recently built house is located on the [9]____ of the city, with good public transportation links. Downstairs there's a kitchen, a living room, and a dining room, while on the [10]____ floor are three bedrooms and a stylish bathroom. Outside the house there are four [11]____ down to a small yard, where there's a [12]____ that is perfect for outdoor entertaining.

9 **a** suburbs **b** outskirts **c** center
10 **a** basement **b** first **c** second
11 **a** steps **b** stairs **c** paths
12 **a** patio **b** basement **c** balcony

Go online for more practice   Go online to check your progress

Practical English Boys' night out

making suggestions

1 MAKING SUGGESTIONS

a Re-order the words to make phrases for making and responding to suggestions.

1 not / why
Why not _____?

2 very / fish / keen / not / I'm / on / raw
_____.

3 a / idea / great / that's
_____!

4 restaurant / don't / sushi / that / we / why / new / try
_____?

5 about / Chinese / having / what / food
_____?

6 shall / lunch / go / we / where / for
_____?

7 cab / could / to / time / get / we / a / save
_____.

8 Italian / to / going / how / an / restaurant / about
_____?

9 there / go / let's
_____.

b Complete the conversation with the phrases from **a**.

Rena	I'm hungry. [1]*Where shall we go for lunch*___?
Phil	I think there's a burger place near here. [2]_____.
Rena	Phil, you know I don't eat meat.
Phil	Oops! Sorry, I forgot. Well, [3]_____? I like pasta.
Rena	Aren't you on a diet?
Phil	Well, yes…
Rena	No pasta for you, then. [4]_____?
Phil	I'm not sure about Japanese food. [5]_____
Rena	Well, [6]_____? I know a place that makes excellent fried rice.
Phil	[7]_____? Is it far from here?
Rena	It's a couple of blocks away. [8]_____.
Phil	[9]_____! Let's do that.

2 VERB FORMS

Complete the sentences with the correct form of a verb from the list.

_____
eat out   go   meet   ~~order~~   play   watch
_____

1 We could *order*_____ a pizza.
2 Let's _____ a movie.
3 What about _____ at 9 p.m.?
4 Why don't we _____ cards?
5 How about _____ to the theater?
6 Let's _____ tonight.

3 SOCIAL ENGLISH

Complete the conversation.

Ellie	Joe?
Joe	Hi, Ellie.
Ellie	It's Mom's birthday, and you're late. Where are you, [1]a*nyway*_____?
Joe	That's [2]wh_____ I'm calling. I'm not going to [3]m_____ it for dinner.
Ellie	Why not?
Joe	I'm at a friend's house. She's [4]o_____ to Canada tomorrow to start her new job, and I wanted to say goodbye.
Ellie	But why tonight? It's [5]n_____ that I don't think you should say goodbye, but couldn't you do it tomorrow?
Joe	Not really. I wanted to have a [6]w_____ with her about something before she left.
Ellie	Mom's going to be upset.
Joe	Sorry, Ellie. It won't [7]h_____ again. Tell Mom I'll see her tomorrow.

Go online to practice the Practical English phrases

1 GRAMMAR

(Circle) the correct words.

1 John and Mary are delighted because their son *gets / 's getting / will get* married next year.
2 He *plays / 's playing / 's been playing* tennis for ten years.
3 You *don't have to / ought to / must not* send text messages when you're driving. It's against the law.
4 I'd love to *can / be able to / could to* play the piano, but I can't.
5 If I *have / had / will have* time tonight, I'll send you those photos.
6 If I knew the answer, I'll tell / tell / 'd tell you.

2 VOCABULARY

(Circle) the word that is different.

1 dishonest   irresponsible   sympathetic   unkind
2 borrow   charge   invest   salary
3 public   elemenatary   private   grade
4 arena   coach   track   stadium
5 cast   extra   plot   star
6 lips   shoulder   teeth   tongue

3 PRONUNCIATION

(Circle) the word with a different sound.

	key	1 **c**arpet **c**ast **c**ircle **c**ritic
	snake	2 **c**eiling **c**enter **c**ozy firepla**c**e
	shower	3 **c**ity musi**c**ian spa**c**ious spe**c**ial
	tr**ai**n	4 st**are** st**a**te t**a**ste tr**ai**ler
	b**i**ke	5 **eye**s f**ai**l h**i**gh sm**i**le

4 GRAMMAR & VOCABULARY

Read the article. (Circle) a, b, or c.

Alternative schooling

Mother-of-two, Sue Cowley, is an experienced teacher and author of many books on how to give children [1]_____ education. These days, teachers [2]_____ the first people to insist that children must be educated at school, not at home. However, Mrs. Cowley doesn't agree. That's why she decided to take her children out of school for six months to go on a road trip. The route the family took [3]_____ by the children themselves, Alvie and Edite, who were eleven and eight at the time.

In November 2014, they [4]_____ in the family car and headed for the Netherlands, where they stayed in a mobile home on the [5]_____ of Amsterdam. They visited Anne Frank's house and the Rijksmuseum. From there, they drove all around Europe before making their way to China. While their [6]_____ were studying hard at school, Alvie and Edite [7]_____ giant pandas at Beijing Zoo.

The children [8]_____ get up early or study on their trip, but their mother [9]_____ them write a page in their travel journal every day. Alvie and Edite learned a lot, including how to draw accurate maps of their travels and what to do if you become separated from your family on the subway.

[10]_____ at school since they returned from their trip, but Mrs. Cowley would like to take them on another adventure one day.

1 **a** better   **b** best   **c** the best
2 **a** are usually   **b** usually are   **c** used to be
3 **a** chose   **b** was chose   **c** was chosen
4 **a** set down   **b** set off   **c** set up
5 **a** coast   **b** outskirts   **c** suburbs
6 **a** classmates   **b** colleagues   **c** partners
7 **a** have visited   **b** had visited   **c** were visiting
8 **a** can't   **b** didn't have to   **c** must not
9 **a** allowed   **b** let   **c** made
10 **a** They're   **b** They've been   **c** They were

✓ **Go online** to check your progress

> People who work sitting down get paid more than people who work standing up.
> *Ogden Nash, US poet*

G choosing between gerunds and infinitives **V** work **P** word stress

1 VOCABULARY work

a Complete the text with words from the list.

applied downsized fired ~~overtime~~ promoted ran
resign retire set up shifts training course

My father's first job was at a small local company. He had to work a lot of ¹ *overtime*, which he really hated, but he knew he would be ² _____ if he didn't do it. One day, he decided to ³ _____ from the job. He ⁴ _____ for a new job with a multinational company. At first, he worked ⁵ _____ in a factory. Then, he got ⁶ _____ to supervisor. Later, he was ⁷ _____ because business was bad. After that, my dad took a ⁸ _____ in business management, and he ⁹ _____ his own business. He ¹⁰ _____ the company for 20 years, and he didn't ¹¹ _____ until he was 68 years old. This photo shows the party they organized for him on his last day.

b Complete the sentences with a preposition and a word from the list.

freelance full-time part-time permanent
~~self-employed~~ temporary unemployed

1 Maxine is a *self-employed* mechanic. She loves working *for* _____ herself.
2 My niece is still _____ school, but she has a _____ job. She only works on Friday evenings and Saturdays.
3 João is _____ his third year of college. He's hoping to get a _____ job as a waiter for the summer to earn some money.
4 Laura is _____ charge of IT at the public library. It's a _____ job – she works from 8 a.m. to 6 p.m. every day.
5 My cousin used to work _____ a large multinational company, but he's been _____ since he was downsized last year.
6 My boyfriend has a _____ job in a bank, and he hopes to stay there until he retires. He's responsible _____ customer loans.
7 My sister is a _____ software developer. She works _____ lots of different companies.

c Complete the sentences with a noun form of the word in **bold**.

1 A _musician_ plays **music** for a living.
2 They're looking for a _____ to **translate** some documents into Chinese.
3 The company **employs** over 200 people – 150 of whom have full-time _____.
4 Hanna studied **pharmacy** because she wanted to be a _____.
5 When we **retire**, we'd like to spend our _____ with our grandchildren.
6 They're going to **promote** someone, but we don't know who's going to get the _____.
7 Ken's interested in **law**, so he'd like to be a _____.
8 My son is good at all the **sciences**, so I'm sure he'll be a _____ when he's older.
9 My colleague tried to **resign**, but our boss wouldn't accept his _____.
10 I **applied** for the job, but I sent in the _____ too late.
11 A _____ has to get up early to take care of his **farm**.
12 He wasn't **qualified** for the job because he didn't have any _____.

d Complete the sentences with the correct form of a word from the list. Use each word twice.

company   fire   market   run   work

1 I like spending time with John. I enjoy his _company_.
2 The track and field official _____ his gun to start the race.
3 I dropped my phone in the bathtub and now it doesn't _____.
4 I _____ five miles every evening.
5 Jane was _____ because she stole money from the company.
6 We always buy fruit and vegetables from our local _____.
7 My sister has applied for a job with an engineering _____.
8 There isn't a big _____ for this kind of product in South America.
9 I _____ part-time in a café.
10 One day, I would like to _____ my own business.

2 PRONUNCIATION word stress

a Underline the stressed syllable.

1 ap|pli|ca|tion
2 a|pply
3 em|ploy|ment
4 down|size
5 far|mer
6 free|lance
7 law|yer
8 mu|si|cian
9 per|ma|nent
10 phar|ma|cist
11 pro|mo|tion
12 qua|li|fi|ca|tion
13 qua|li|fy
14 re|sig|na|tion
15 re|tire
16 re|tire|ment
17 sci|en|tist
18 tem|po|ra|ry
19 trans|la|tion
20 un|em|ployed

b 🔊 8.1 Listen and check. Then listen again and repeat.

3 GRAMMAR choosing between gerunds and infinitives

a Circle a, b, or c.

1 It's difficult _____ a good job these days.
   a finding **b** to find **c** find
2 He isn't very good at _____ decisions.
   a making **b** to make **c** make
3 They promised _____ me at the end of the month.
   a paying **b** to pay **c** pay
4 I should _____. It's getting late.
   a going **b** to go **c** go
5 _____ an application form can take ages.
   a Filling out **b** To fill out **c** Fill out
6 My girlfriend told me _____ her later.
   a calling **b** to call **c** call
7 The movie I saw last night made me _____.
   a crying **b** to cry **c** cry
8 Tim really enjoys _____ on a team.
   a working **b** to work **c** work
9 I went to the supermarket _____ some bread.
   a buying **b** to buy **c** buy
10 I gave up _____ basketball when I went to college.
   a playing **b** to play **c** play

b Correct any mistakes in the highlighted verbs. Check (✔) the correct sentences.

1 I remember having my first job interview. I was really nervous! ✔

2 Lift heavy weights can give you back problems.
  Lifting heavy weights

3 The interviewer asked me wait in the reception area.

4 I know you don't like my boyfriend, but please try to be nice to him.

5 Go on, tell me! I promise to not laugh.

6 The bus didn't come, so we started walking home.

7 Anna continued study until midnight.

8 It's impossible to read your writing!

9 If you're tired, I don't mind stay in tonight.

10 Everyone is afraid of being fired.

c Complete the sentences with the correct form of the verbs in parentheses.

1 I went to the bank *to get*_____ some money. (get)
2 Try _____ to your boss. She might be able to help you. (talk)
3 I want you _____ me exactly what happened. (tell)
4 I didn't remember _____ the stove, so the kitchen was full of smoke. (turn off)
5 Some couples can go on _____ to each other for days after an argument. (not speak)
6 I'm going out with Jamie because he makes me _____. (laugh)
7 _____ drive is one of the requirements of the job. (be able to)
8 The service had been so bad that the manager agreed _____ us for our meal. (not charge)

Go online for more practice

Have a nice day!

Buy less, choose well, make it last.
Vivienne Westwood, British fashion designer

G reported speech: sentences and questions | **V** shopping, making nouns from verbs | **P** the letters *ai*

1 GRAMMAR reported speech

a Circle the correct words.

1 Matt said yesterday that he *will* / *would* come shopping with me.

2 We asked the salesperson how much *it was* / *was it*.

3 My sister *said me* / *told me* that she had spent all her money at the sale.

4 I asked Lucy where *she bought* / *did she buy* her clothes.

5 You told me that you *may* / *might* go shopping on Saturday.

6 My brother asked me *if I can* / *if I could* lend him some money to buy a new video game.

7 Kate said that she *had to* / *must* go to the supermarket.

8 I asked my sister whether *suited me the dress* / *the dress suited me*, and she said I looked great!

9 Carolina asked me what *I wanted* / *did I want* from the mall.

10 Nick said that he couldn't pay me back, because he *has forgotten* / *had forgotten* his wallet.

b Complete the sentences with *said* or *told.*

1 Jackie *said* that she was thinking of buying a new car.

2 My boyfriend _____ me he wanted to see his friends more often.

3 You _____ you'd check the price online.

4 I _____ you I might be late.

5 Ryan _____ me that he couldn't find his credit card.

6 My sister _____ that she would buy me a new smartphone for my birthday.

c Report the conversations.

1 "Where do you buy your clothes?"
"I buy them online."
I asked Kate *where she bought her clothes* _____.
She told *me (that) she bought them online* _____.

2 "Have you seen my wallet?"
"I don't know where it is."
He asked me _____.
I said _____.

3 "Do your snow boots still fit you?"
"They fit me perfectly!"
I asked my daughter _____.
She told _____.

4 "How much did you pay for your jacket?"
"It was a bargain."
I asked Ji-ho _____.
He said _____.

5 "Where are you going tomorrow?"
"I'm meeting some friends."
Sophie asked me _____.
I told _____.

6 "Do you need anything from the supermarket?"
"I want some chocolate."
I asked John _____.
He said _____.

7 "Did you enjoy your stay?"
"It's been very enjoyable."
She asked us _____.
We told _____.

8 "When are you going shopping?"
"I may go on Saturday."
Holly asked me _____.
I said _____.

2 VOCABULARY shopping, making nouns from verbs

a Complete the pairs of sentences with the correct word, a or b.

1 The sports section is on the top floor of the __b__.
   You can find this __a__ in shopping malls all over the world.
   a chain store **b** department store

2 He wasn't happy with his new pants, so he asked for a ____.
   She paid with a twenty-dollar bill, so the salesperson gave her some change with her ____.
   a receipt **b** refund

3 Those pants are too short – they don't ____ you.
   That dress is the right size, but it really doesn't ____ you.
   a fit **b** suit

4 You can go to a ____ to buy your favorite author's latest novel.
   Instead of buying the book, she's going to borrow it from the ____.
   a bookstore **b** library

5 The whole family comes with me when I do the weekly shopping, and the children take turns pushing the ____.
   I only needed a few things, so I picked up a ____ at the entrance to the store.
   a basket **b** cart

6 This leather jacket was only $100. What a ____!
   There was a 50% ____ on sandals, so I bought two pairs.
   a bargain **b** discount

7 I'd ____ a coat if I were you – it's cold outside.
   It would be a good idea to ____ that shirt before you buy it.
   a try on **b** put on

8 You use a ____ when you want to pay at the end of the month.
   There's no extra charge if you pay by ____.
   a credit card **b** debit card

b Complete the sentences with the noun form of the verbs in parentheses.

1 The company reported a _loss_ of two million dollars last year. (lose)

2 The _____ was very slow, so we didn't leave a tip. (serve)

3 Selina gets special _____ because she's the manager's niece. (treat)

4 We couldn't reach an _____ with our boss about salaries. (agree)

5 My exam grades this semester are a big _____ on last semester. (improve)

6 They had an _____, and they aren't talking to each other. (argue)

7 They had to get a _____ of their house before they could sell it. (value)

8 His greatest _____ was winning an Olympic gold medal. (achieve)

9 It's a difficult _____ to make between my best friend's wedding or my sister's birthday party. (choose)

10 The restaurant had to close because of bad _____. (manage)

11 There's a _____ on Saturday against the closure of the hospital. (demonstrate)

12 I bought two shirts and a pair of shorts at the end-of-summer _____ at the mall. (sell)

13 After careful _____, we've decided to sell the company. (consider)

14 My attempt to run a marathon ended in _____ when I fell and broke my leg after the first mile. (fail)

15 I had to resist the _____ to have another cupcake – they were delicious! (tempt)

c Complete the text with the noun form of the verbs in parentheses.

A month ago, I bought a video game online for my son's birthday. I got a confirmation email back, which said that ¹_delivery_ (deliver) would take about ten days. Two weeks later, I began to worry. I knew the seller had received my ²_____ (pay), but the video game hadn't arrived. So I decided to make a ³_____ (complain). I sent an email to the seller with a copy of the order confirmation as an ⁴_____ (attach). I received a ⁵_____ (respond) immediately, which said that the seller would look into the incident. After that, I heard nothing for three days, so I sent another email demanding an ⁶_____ (explain). This time I had more ⁷_____ (succeed), and the seller said he would send another copy of the game. If I don't receive it before my son's birthday, I'm going to ask for ⁸_____ (compensate).

3 PRONUNCIATION the letters *ai*

a Circle the word where *ai* is pronounced differently.

1 barg**ai**n mount**ai**n cl**ai**m
2 **ai**r compl**ai**n r**ai**n
3 p**ai**nting s**ai**d w**ai**t
4 **ai**rline f**ai**r r**ai**lway
5 capt**ai**n pl**ai**n em**ai**l
6 br**ai**n h**ai**r st**ai**rs

b ▶ 8.2 Listen and check. Then listen again and repeat the words.

9A Lucky encounters

G third conditional   **V** making adjectives and adverbs   **P** sentence rhythm, weak pronunciation of *have*

1 GRAMMAR third conditional

a Complete the sentences with *had* or *would have.*

1 If I'd known it was your birthday, I*'d have* _____ bought you a present.

2 It _____ been quicker if we'd gone by train. Our flight was very delayed.

3 Ahmet wouldn't have been late for work if the bus _____ been on time.

4 I'm sure that if David _____ seen you, he would have said hello.

5 I _____ gone to their party if they'd invited me, but they didn't.

6 If you'd got up earlier, you _____ had time to make your bed.

7 If Kim _____ paid attention in class, she would have known about the exam.

8 You wouldn't have fallen asleep at the movie theater if you _____ had a nap this afternoon.

b Complete the sentences with the correct form of the verbs in parentheses.

1 If you'd told me you weren't staying for dinner, I *wouldn't have made* so much food. (not make)

2 We _____ on time if we'd left half an hour earlier. (arrive)

3 If we _____ a table, we wouldn't have been able to have dinner there. (not book)

4 You'd have seen my message if you _____ your cell phone. (check)

5 I would have enjoyed the party more if the music _____ so loud. (not be)

6 If you'd concentrated on what you were doing, you _____ so many mistakes. (not make)

7 If I _____ it was going to be so cold today, I would have worn a warmer coat. (know)

8 We _____ Joe to dinner if we'd known you didn't like him. (not invite)

9 If you _____ so rude about my mother, I wouldn't have gotten so angry. (not be)

10 My sister _____ promoted if she'd refused to work overtime. (not get)

c Complete the second sentence so it has a similar meaning to the first sentence.

1 I got to the restaurant late because I went to the wrong place first.
If I hadn't gone to the wrong place first, *I wouldn't have gotten to the restaurant late.*

2 I passed my final exams, so I graduated from college.
I wouldn't have graduated from college if _____
_____ .

3 Helen didn't have the right qualifications, so she didn't get the job.
If Helen had had the right qualifications, _____
_____ .

4 We had lunch before we left, so we weren't hungry.
We would have been hungry if _____
_____ .

5 We didn't play tennis this afternoon because it was windy.
If it hadn't been so windy this afternoon, _____
_____ .

6 You got lost because you didn't follow my directions.
You wouldn't have gotten lost if _____
_____ .

7 I didn't win that game because you cheated.
If you hadn't cheated, _____
_____ .

8 Alex wasn't very careful with his glasses, so he broke them.
If Alex had been more careful with his glasses, _____
_____ .

2 PRONUNCIATION sentence rhythm, weak pronunciation of *have*

a ◑ 9.1 Listen and complete the sentences.

1 If they hadn't played so badly in the second half, they *would have won* _____ the game.

2 If you'd told me about the meeting, I _____.

3 She _____ the coat if it hadn't been so expensive.

4 If there had been room for us, we _____ the night.

5 We _____ to the movie theater on time if we'd taken a taxi.

6 If I'd known you were moving to a new house, I _____ you.

b Listen again and repeat the sentences. Copy the rhythm.

3 VOCABULARY making adjectives and adverbs

a Complete the chart with the two adjective forms of each noun from the list.

care ~~comfort~~ fortune luck patience

	+	−
adjective ending in -*able*	[1] *comfortable*	[2] *uncomfortable*
adjective ending in -*ate*	[3]	[4]
adjective ending in -*ful* / *less*	[5]	[6]
adjective ending in -*ient*	[7]	[8]
adjective ending in -*y*	[9]	[10]

b Complete the sentences with the correct form of the words in parentheses.

1 We were sitting *comfortably* on the sofa when there was a knock at the door. (comfort)

2 I was in a hurry, so I waited _____ for the elevator to arrive. (patience)

3 She put down the glass _____, so it fell on the floor and broke. (care)

4 _____, I'd taken an umbrella because it began to rain before I'd gotten to my office. (fortune)

5 They were _____ to lose the basketball game because they'd played very well. (luck)

c Complete the charts.

	adjectives	
noun	**+**	**−**
success	[1] *successful*	[2] *unsuccessful*
possibility	[3]	[4]
self	[5]	[6]
use	[7]	[8]
suit	[9]	[10]

	adverbs	
noun	**+**	**−**
success	[11] *successfully*	[12] *unsuccessfully*
possibility	[13]	[14]
self	[15]	[16]
use	[17]	[18]
suit	[19]	[20]

d Complete the sentences with a word from the charts.

1 It's *possible* to see the English coast from France on a clear day.

2 She very _____ took both of the cookies that were left on the plate.

3 You should throw that old umbrella away – it's completely _____.

4 All of their children have been very _____ in their chosen careers.

5 They wore sandals and shorts in the snow! They were very _____ dressed for the weather.

e Complete the text with the correct adjective or adverb of the nouns in parentheses.

Unlucky teen's meeting with an alligator

An American teenager made a [1]*careless* (care) mistake yesterday when he jumped into a river without checking the area for alligators before going swimming.

Kaleb Langdale was at the Caloosahatchee River in Florida with friends when he decided to go for a swim. The [2]_____ (patient) young man soon found himself in the [3]_____ (comfort) position of sharing the water with an alligator, which started to attack him. He was [4]_____ (luck) enough to escape the first attack and began to swim to the bank, where his friends were [5]_____ (desperation) waiting for him. [6]_____ (fortune), the ten-foot animal attacked again, and this time it held on to Kaleb's arm. [7]_____ (luck), Kaleb managed to get away, but his arm was seriously injured in the process.

Kaleb is now recovering in the hospital, and doctors say his condition is [8]_____ (comfort) despite his injuries. He recommends that anybody who goes swimming in the Caloosahatchee River should check the area [9]_____ (care) before going swimming.

Go online for more practice

G quantifiers   **V** electronic devices   **P** linking, *ough* and *augh*

1 VOCABULARY electronic devices

a Complete the words.

1 k <u>e</u> y b <u>o</u> <u>a</u> r d

2 p _ _ _ t _ _

3 s _ _ _ k _ _

4 a _ _ p _ _ r

5 r _ m _ _ _ _
 c _ _ t _ _ l

6 o _ _ l _ _

7 ch _ _ g _ _

8 s _ _ t _ _

9 p _ _ g

10 U _ _
 c _ b _ _

11 f _ _ _ h
 d _ _ _ e

12 r _ _ t _ _

b Complete the sentences with a word from **a**.

1 Let's turn the lights on. Where's the <u>switch</u>?
2 I have the presentation on a _____ _____, so I don't need to take my laptop.
3 My battery's getting low. Can I borrow your _____?
4 Can I use your _____? I need to print out the boarding pass for my flight.
5 You'll need a _____ _____ if you want to connect your phone to your laptop.
6 Where's the "@" symbol on this _____?
7 Who has the _____ _____ for the TV? I want to change channels.
8 You can't use American plugs in the UK if you don't have an _____.
9 If you turn on the _____, you might be able to hear something!
10 Is the _____ working? I don't have an internet connection.
11 Never take a _____ out of an _____ with wet hands – you might get an electric shock.

c Complete the crossword.

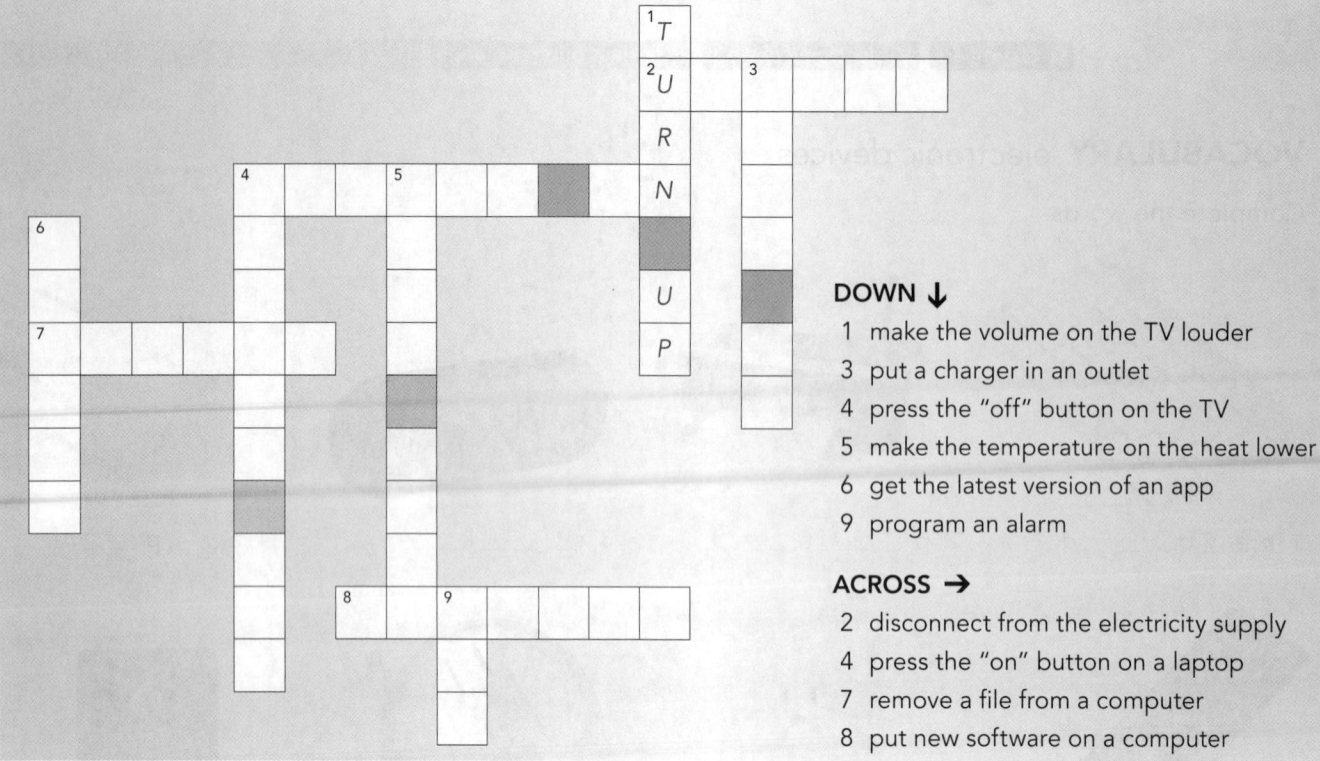

DOWN ↓
1 make the volume on the TV louder
3 put a charger in an outlet
4 press the "off" button on the TV
5 make the temperature on the heat lower
6 get the latest version of an app
9 program an alarm

ACROSS →
2 disconnect from the electricity supply
4 press the "on" button on a laptop
7 remove a file from a computer
8 put new software on a computer

2 GRAMMAR quantifiers

a Circle the correct answers. One, two, or three answers may be correct.

1 Do you eat ____ cookies?
   a many
   b a lot of
   c much

2 I sleep ____ when I'm on vacation.
   a a lot of
   b a lot
   c lots of

3 I don't drink ____ coffee.
   a many
   b a lot of
   c much

4 You can sit here. There's ____ room.
   a many
   b much
   c plenty of

5 My sister has ____ friends.
   a a lot of
   b lots of
   c many

6 Can I have ____ more cake please?
   It's delicious!
   a a few
   b a little
   c very little

7 My phone has ____ games because I never play them.
   a a few
   b very few
   c very little

8 There are ____ young people living in their own homes than there used to be.
   a fewer
   b less
   c little

9 I can't hear you. There's ____ noise.
   a enough
   b too many
   c too much

10 You aren't working ____.
   a hard enough
   b enough hard
   c too much hard

11 There isn't ____ milk in the refrigerator.
   a any
   b no
   c some

12 A How much bread is there?
   B ____. I finished it all.
   a Any
   b None
   c No any

b Complete each pair of sentences so that they have the same meaning. More than one answer may be possible.

1 There *aren't enough* chairs.
  There are *too few* chairs.

2 He can't afford it. He doesn't have _____ money.
  He can't afford it. It's _____ for him.

3 We only had _____ sleep last night.
  We didn't have _____ sleep last night.

4 There are _____ cars in the parking garage.
  There aren't _____ parking spaces.

5 There's _____ gas in the tank.
  There isn't _____ gas in the tank.

6 She buys very _____ books these days.
  She doesn't buy _____ books these days.

c Complete the sentences with a quantifier and the words in parentheses. Sometimes more than one answer is possible.

1 The party was a disaster. There weren't *many people*. (people)
2 I didn't have _____, so I only ordered a plate of French fries. (money)
3 We'll have to drive. There aren't _____ on Sundays. (buses)
4 It's raining, so there are _____ on the beach – just one or two. (people)
5 He can't drive yet. He isn't _____. (old)
6 Anna's worried because she's a freelance photographer, and she has _____ right now. (work)
7 You can't move in their living room. There's _____. (furniture)
8 We can't use the printer. There's _____. (paper)
9 It took us a long time to get here. There was _____. (traffic)
10 I couldn't sleep on the plane. There were _____. (children)
11 I'll only be a minute. I have to make _____ before we leave. (phone calls)
12 This jacket doesn't fit me. It's _____. (small)

3 PRONUNCIATION linking, *ough* and *augh*

a ◑9.2 Listen and write the sentences.

1 I *switched it on*.   5 I _____.
2 I _____.   6 I _____.
3 I _____.   7 I _____.
4 I _____.   8 I _____.

b ◑9.2 Listen again and repeat the sentences. Try to link the words.

c Circle the word with a different sound.

1 saw	2 up	3 saw	4 saw
brought	cough	bought	caught
(although)	enough	daughter	laughed
thought	tough	through	taught

d ◑9.3 Listen and check. Then listen again and repeat the words.

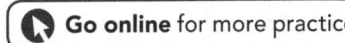

Go online for more practice   Go online to check your progress

1 INDIRECT QUESTIONS

a Circle the correct words.

1 Can you tell me what time *it is* / *is it*, please?
2 Do you know if this bus *does go* / *goes* to the airport?
3 Could you tell me where *can I* / *I can* buy a ticket?
4 I wonder where *Lola is* / *is Lola* today.
5 Do you know whether this shirt *does come* / *comes* in a larger size?
6 I'd like to know where *are you* / *you're* going.
7 I wonder what time *the restaurant closes* / *does the restaurant close*.
8 Can you remember who *did you speak to* / *you spoke to*?

b Make questions 1–6 more indirect by using the beginnings given.

1 What time is the next bus for Boston?
   I'd like to know *what time the next bus for Boston is.*
2 What time does it arrive?
   Do you know _____?
3 Which stop does the bus go from?
   Could you tell me _____?
4 How much does a one-way ticket cost?
   Could you tell me _____?
5 Do I need to change buses?
   I wonder _____.
6 Do I get a 20% discount with a student ID?
   Can you tell me _____?

c Complete the conversation with the indirect questions from **a**. There is one question you don't need to use.

Ticket agent Can I help you?
Max Yes, please. ¹ *I'd like to know what time the next bus for Boston is.*
Ticket agent Well, the next bus leaves at 10 a.m.
Max Great. ² _____
Ticket agent Sure. It costs $35.95.
Max ³ _____
Ticket agent Yes, you do. That means it'll cost you $28.75.
Max OK. Here's my student ID…and my credit card.
Ticket agent And here's your ticket.
Max Thanks. ⁴ _____.
Ticket agent No, you don't. The bus goes straight through.
Max And ⁵ _____
Ticket agent Yes, it gets to Boston at 2:20 p.m.
Max Thanks a lot.

3 SOCIAL ENGLISH

Complete the conversation with the words and phrases from the list.

either   I guess   It's obvious   Of course   ~~Stop it!~~
What if

A ¹ *Stop it!* _____ You keep yawning. Everyone will think you're bored.
B Oh, sorry. ² _____ I'm a little tired.
A ³ _____ you're tired. You've had a long day.
B Well, I did get up at six o'clock this morning.
A Oh, come on. Let's go. ⁴ _____ you aren't enjoying the party.
B I'm sorry. I think I need to go to bed.
A I know. ⁵ _____ we go home and do something fun tomorrow?
B That sounds like a great idea. And I promise I'll be more fun and I won't yawn all day, ⁶ _____.
A Good!

Go online to practice the Practical English phrases

1 GRAMMAR

Complete the sentences with the correct form of the verbs in parentheses. Add additional words if needed.

1 I _____ my girlfriend for three years. We met when we were in college. (know)

2 When I was a child, I _____ like big dogs – they frightened me. (used to)

3 I'm not sure, but I think that man _____ Susan's brother. (be)

4 If I lived downtown, I _____ to work instead of driving. (walk)

5 Jake's room is a mess, and he refuses _____ it. (clean)

6 The police officer asked the man where he _____ the day before. (be)

2 VOCABULARY

Circle the word that is different.

1 duck   mussels   shrimp   squid

2 colleague   couple   roommate   partner

3 comedy   script   thriller   western

4 degree   public   private   religious

5 attic   basement   gate   first floor

6 apply for   be downsized   resign   retire

3 PRONUNCIATION

Circle the word with a different sound.

↑ up	1 **cour**se en**ou**gh l**u**cky t**o**ngue
ɔr horse	2 c**our**t d**oor** sc**ore** w**or**k
OU phone	3 alth**ough** r**ou**ter thr**ow** t**oe**s
u boot	4 fl**oor** r**oof** s**ui**t thr**ough**
ɑ clock	5 c**o**nfident l**o**bster n**o**se w**a**tch

4 GRAMMAR & VOCABULARY

Read the article. Circle a, b, or c.

DANGEROUS DEVICES

Most of us would agree that computers and smartphones [1]____ made life easier for us. However, there are a [2]____ people who might not think the same because they've [3]____ injured by their electronic devices. Experts are becoming increasingly worried [4]____ this problem. One of the [5]____ dangerous devices appears to be phone chargers. You probably [6]____ be injured if you use your original charger, but fake chargers are different. Fake chargers are sold at much lower prices than originals, and when customers choose [7]____ them, they're often tempted to buy the cheaper of the two. They think they've found a [8]____ because they've spent very little money [9]____ it. It's thought that a woman died recently because of a fake charger. She had plugged [10]____ the charger and attached her phone before she tried to make a phone call. Unfortunately, she received a massive electric shock from the charger, and she [11]____ killed instantly. Phone companies say that she [12]____ have died if she hadn't used a fake charger.

1 **a** are	**b** had	**c** have
2 **a** few	**b** less	**c** little
3 **a** be	**b** been	**c** was
4 **a** about	**b** in	**c** of
5 **a** less	**b** more	**c** most
6 **a** don't	**b** not	**c** won't
7 **a** between	**b** from	**c** to
8 **a** bargain	**b** bill	**c** budget
9 **a** about	**b** in	**c** on
10 **a** in	**b** on	**c** out
11 **a** is	**b** was	**c** were
12 **a** didn't	**b** won't	**c** wouldn't

✓ **Go online** to check your progress

When you become a celebrity, the world owns you and your image.
Megan Fox, American actress

G relative clauses: defining and nondefining   **V** compound nouns   **P** word stress

1 GRAMMAR relative clauses

a Complete the sentences with a relative pronoun. Where two answers are possible, write both pronouns.

1 What's the name of the city *where* you can see Taj Mahal?
2 Apple is the company *which / that* makes the iPhone.
3 Who's the actor _____ wife died in a skiing accident?
4 The thing _____ my son wants most for his birthday is a bike.
5 Helen Sharman was the first British woman _____ went into space.
6 That's the restaurant _____ we celebrated my dad's 80th birthday.
7 Alexander Graham Bell is the man _____ invented the telephone.
8 What's the name of your friend _____ parents have a huge house in the country?
9 Mountain View, California, is the city _____ Google is based.
10 Amazon is the company _____ has the largest number of online sales in the world.

b In which sentence in **a** can you leave out the relative pronoun?

c Cross out the extra word in each of the sentences.

1 Those are the students who ~~they~~ won the competition.
2 Isn't he the actor who he played the role of Sherlock Holmes?
3 Why don't we stay in the hotel where we stayed there last year?
4 I always use the supermarket that it is closest to where I live.
5 She's the woman whose her daughter went to the same school as me.
6 What's the name of the store where you bought your jacket there?
7 That's the computer that it isn't working.
8 This is the show I was telling you about it.
9 These are the boots I bought them last Saturday.
10 That's the woman whose car we bought it.

d Complete the sentences with a relative pronoun and the phrases from the list. You will need to leave out one of the words in each of the phrases.

~~he plays the part of Jon Snow in *Game of Thrones*~~
it is in the Himalayas
her husband is a Spanish soccer player
the *Mona Lisa* can be seen there
it was opened in China in 2011
she helped hundreds of slaves to escape

1 Kit Harington, *who plays the part of Jon Snow in* Game *of Thrones*, was born in London.

2 The Louvre, _____, is in the center of Paris.

3 Mount Everest, _____, is the world's highest mountain.

4 Jiaozhou Bay Bridge, _____, is the longest bridge in the world.

5 Shakira, _____, is originally from Colombia.

6 Harriet Tubman, _____, has been chosen to appear on the $20 bill.

2 VOCABULARY compound nouns

a Complete the compound nouns.

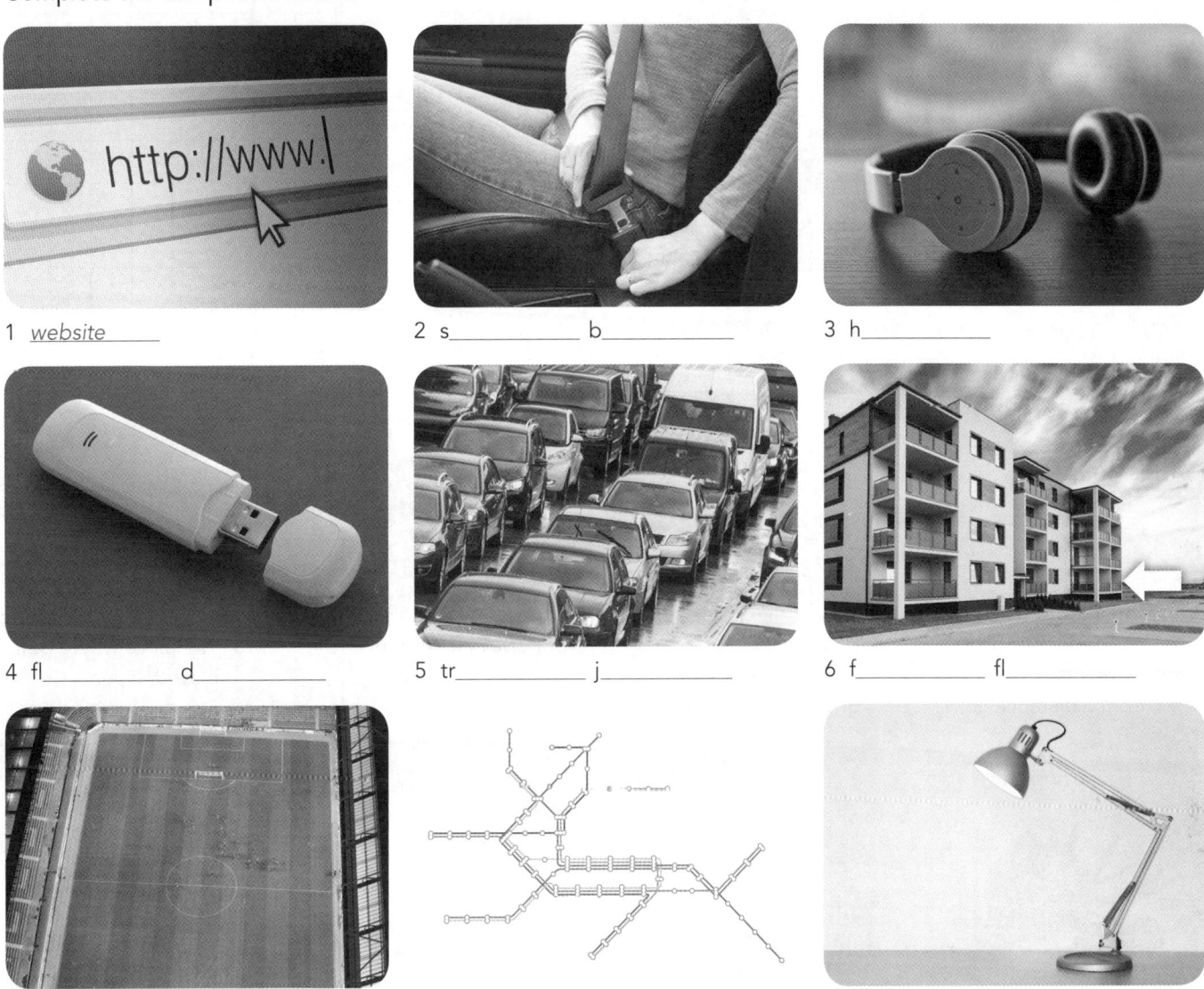

1 *website*

2 s_____ b_____

3 h_____

4 fl_____ d_____

5 tr_____ j_____

6 f_____ fl_____

7 s_____ f_____

8 s_____ m_____

9 d_____ l_____

b Match a word from **A** to a word from **B** to make compound nouns. Then complete the sentences.

| A | ~~bank~~ | bicycle | high | room | rush | science | sound | speed | top | training |

| B | ~~account~~ | camera | course | fiction | floor | hour | lane | mate | school | track |

1 My salary is deposited directly into my *bank account* every month.
2 They live on the _____, so they have a great view of the city.
3 I love the _____ of the latest *Star Wars* movie – I listen to it all the time.
4 My brother is taking a _____ to learn about health and safety.
5 Do you get along well with your _____ or do you argue about paying the bills?
6 The first year of _____ in the US is usually ninth grade.
7 Bike riders should use the _____ to keep away from traffic.
8 Commuters usually travel to work during _____.
9 All the drivers are slowing down because there's a _____ up ahead.
10 I really like fantasy movies, but my favorite genre is _____.

c Complete the word puzzle and find the missing compound noun.

|¹N|U|R|S|E|R|Y| |S|C|H|O|O|L|

(crossword grid with numbered clues 1–10)

1 A school for children ages two to five. (7, 6)

2 Water that comes through pipes and isn't sold in bottles. (3, 5)

3 A device for controling equipment such as the TV from a distance. (6, 7)

4 Illusions created in a movie by computer graphics, etc. (7, 7)

5 Repairs to streets and freeways. (4, 4)

6 The place where golf is played. (4, 6)

7 A product you can use for frying food or putting on salads. (5, 3)

8 You can send this to a friend if you don't want to call them. (4, 7)

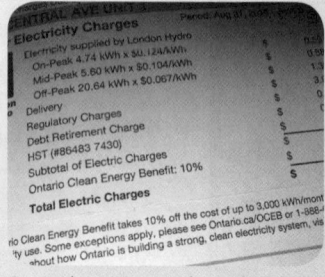

9 A document that shows how much you owe your energy company. (11, 4)

10 A place where people can watch sports indoors, like basketball or hockey. (6, 5)

3 PRONUNCIATION word stress

a Match 1–8 to the words in the list to make compound nouns.

board   court   ticket   lights   ~~products~~   school   page   tone

1 clean|ing _products_
2 key _____
3 pro|file _____
4 par|king _____
5 ring _____
6 e|le|men|tary _____
7 te|nnis _____
8 tra|ffic _____

b 🔊10.1 Listen and check. Then listen again and repeat the words. <u>U</u>nderline the stressed syllables.

Go online for more practice

And the murderer is...

Behind every crime is a story of sadness.
Enrique Peña Nieto, Mexican president

G tag questions **V** crime **P** intonation in tag questions

1 VOCABULARY crime

a Order the letters to make words that complete the sentences.

1 A *murder* (urmrde) was committed last night.
2 _____ (tecesdetiv) are investigating the crime.
3 They're hoping to _____ (vesol) it as soon as possible.
4 The _____ (vticim) was the wife of a millionaire.
5 The main _____ (pecsusts) are the woman's husband, their son, and their driver.
6 _____ (neswitses) say they heard gun shots at around 10 p.m.
7 The police are convinced that the son is the _____ (dermurer).
8 They're currently looking for more _____ (denevice).
9 They need to be able to _____ (ovepr) that they've caught the right person.

b Complete the text with the words from **a**.

NEWS	ENTERTAINMENT	TECH	LIFESTYLE	SPORTS

Murder investigation after body found next to road

Police appeal after murder of man in Millbrook

¹*Detectives* are investigating a ²_____ in Millbrook. The ³_____ was a 26-year-old man, whose body was found last night next to a quiet, back road. No ⁴_____ was found at the scene, and police are appealing to ⁵_____ who saw the man yesterday to help them with their investigation. They believe that the ⁶_____ was someone known to the man. The main ⁷_____ are the man's roommate, his girlfriend, and a neighbor. These people are currently being interviewed by the police in an attempt to ⁸_____ the crime. A police spokesperson said that they had a theory, but so far, they had been unable to ⁹_____ who had committed the crime.

2 GRAMMAR tag questions

a Circle the correct words.

1 You live in Seattle, *don't you* / *aren't you*?
2 But you weren't born in Seattle, *weren't you* / *were you*?
3 You moved to Seattle when you were ten, *weren't you* / *didn't you*?
4 So you've been living here for 20 years, *haven't you* / *have you*?
5 But you're moving to Los Angeles next month, *won't you* / *aren't you*?
6 Your brother lives there, *doesn't he* / *does he*?
7 You've been in prison before, *aren't you* / *haven't you*?
8 I guess you'd like to call your lawyer now, *would you* / *wouldn't you*?

b Complete the tag questions.

1 Adam's living with his parents, *isn't he*?
2 You don't like animals, _____?
3 It isn't difficult, _____?
4 Anthony works in Seoul, _____?
5 They left yesterday, _____?
6 Kathy hasn't come home yet, _____?
7 I'm late, _____?
8 You'll see him tomorrow, _____?
9 I wouldn't like that movie, _____?
10 You haven't had lunch yet, _____?

c Rewrite the sentences using tag questions.

1 I think your sister's in my class.
   Your sister's in my class, isn't she?
2 I'm sure you're younger than me.
   _____?
3 I have a feeling you don't like cheese.
   _____?
4 I heard your brother lives abroad.
   _____?
5 Is it right that you studied physics?
   _____?
6 I'm sure we've been here before.
   _____?
7 I'm sure you wouldn't do that.
   _____?
8 I'm hoping the flight won't be canceled.
   _____?

3 PRONUNCIATION intonation in tag questions

◐10.2 Listen and repeat the sentences. <u>Copy the rhythm</u>.

1 You **called** me **last night**, **didn't you**?
2 He's **older** than **you**, **isn't he**?
3 They **aren't coming tonight**, **are they**?
4 We **missed** the last **bus**, **didn't we**?
5 She'll be **late**, **won't she**?
6 I **can't dance** very **well**, **can I**?
7 We **had** a **great vacation** in **Rio**, **didn't we**?
8 You've **never been** to the **opera before**, **have you**?
9 **That movie** was **really boring**, **wasn't it**?

⬤ Go online for more practice   **✓ Go online** to check your progress

OXFORD
UNIVERSITY PRESS

198 Madison Avenue
New York, NY 10016 USA

Great Clarendon Street, Oxford, OX2 6DP, United Kingdom

Oxford University Press is a department of the University of Oxford.
It furthers the University's objective of excellence in research, scholarship,
and education by publishing worldwide. Oxford is a registered trade
mark of Oxford University Press in the UK and in certain other countries

ISBN: 978 0 19 490668 5

Printed in China

This book is printed on paper from certified and well-managed sources

ACKNOWLEDGMENTS

Back cover photograph: Oxford University Press building/David Fisher

The authors would like to thank all the teachers and students around the world whose feedback has helped us to shape this series.

The authors would also like to thank: all those at Oxford University Press (both in Oxford and around the world) and the design team who have contributed their skills and ideas to producing this course.

Finally very special thanks from Clive to Maria Angeles, Lucia, and Eric, and from Christina to Cristina, for all their support and encouragement. Christina would also like to thank her children Joaquin, Marco, and Krysia for their constant inspiration.

The publisher would like to thank the following for their permission to reproduce photographs: Cover: Hobbit/Shutterstock. Alamy pp.4 (boiled egg/studiomode, vegetables/Stanley Hare), 7 (Blend Images), 9 (women in park/Montgomery Martin), 11 (foodfolio), 17 (rugby/Jonathan Larsen/Diadem Images, man eating/Igor Kardasov), 18 (1/Alex Segre, 2/Mk_Malin, 6/imageBROKER, 7/Peter Titmuss, 9/Bailey-Cooper Photography), 31 (backpackers/Anna Berkut), 44 (4/PBWPIX, 6/D. Hurst), 53 (Li Xin/Xinhua), 54 (mechanic/Image Source), 62 (river/Jeff Greenberg, alligator/James Schwabel), 63 (12), 66 (Robert Clayton), 68 (Kit Harington in Game of Thrones, 2012, The Ghost of Harrenhal/Photo 12, Shakira/dpa picture alliance, Harriet Tubman/Science History Images), 70 (9/Jonny White, 10/Russell Mills), 71 (police line/George Impey, field/Newspix); Getty Images pp.4 (potato/Dave King, chicken/Jon Whitaker), 9 (woman at vending machine, couple doing dishes), 17 (winning couple/Tanya Constantine, whale/Daniela Dirscherl), 18 (commuter train/ Justin Sullivan), 18 (delivery van/Zoomstudio/E+), 18 (train platform/Daniel Kieslinger / EyeEm), 18 (subway/Dong Wenjie), 25 (Imgorthand), 32 (F1 track/ Karim Sahib/AFP, football stadium/SambaPhoto/Eduardo Queiroga – Lumiar), 34 (embrace/Ryan Pierse, Wimbledon All England Lawn Tennis Club Men's Final 2008), 36 (party), 39 (Ethan Miller/Getty Images for Keep Memory Alive), 40 (Steven Spielberg/Samir Hussein/WireImage, poster/Jaws 1975/Universal History Archive/UIG), 44 (3/William Radcliffe, 5/Juan Silva), 48 (unruly students/Big Cheese Photo), 54 (retirement), 69 (7/Jason Hawkes), 70 (sports arena/Tim Clayton - Corbis / Contributor); Oxford University Press pp.4 (salmon, fried egg), 44 (1, 7, 8, 9), 63 (1–3, 5, 8, 10-11), 63 (iphone charger/Catherine Johnson/OUP); Rex Shutterstock pp.42 (The Revenant 2015 poster/20th Century Fox/Regency Enterprises/Kobal, The Revenant 2015 still/20th Century Fox/Regency Enterprises/Kobal), 68 (Qingdao Jiaozhou Bay Bridge/KeystoneUSA-ZUMA); Shutterstock pp. 5 (Asian tea/mama_mia), 9 (couple with tablet), 9 (Couple heading to work/LightField Studios), 12, 13, 16 (both), 17 (hamster, cold woman), 20, 22, 23, 27, 28, 29 (business man/Monkey Business Images), 30 (Venice), 30 (female singer/Milan Ilic Photographer), 32 (pool, tennis, golf, ski slope, running track), 36 (college students/Daniel M Ernst), 37, 41, 44 (2), 45 (couple cooking/AndriyShevchuk), 46, 47 (private high school/New Africa), 47 (female student), 50 (all), 51 (log cabin/Artazum), 51 (home/Lindasj22), 56, 57, 58, 59, 63 (Adapter/ fatir29), 63 (wall outlet/ Gvais), 63 (2 prong/ apisit panyaka), 63 (router/ Proxima Studio), 67, 68 (Louvre, Everest), 69 (1–6, 9), 69 ((subway map/Mihael Mihalev), 70 (1-8).

Pronunciation chart artwork: by Ellis Nadler

Illustrations by: Satoshi Hashimoto/Dutch Uncle p.15 (1–7); John Haslam pp.15 (8), 43, 60, 61, 72; Roger Penwill pp.14, 19, 26, 35, 65; Laura Perez/Anna Goodson Illustration Agency p.44.

Although every effort has been made to trace and contact copyright holders before publication, this has not been possible in some cases. We apologise for any apparent infringement of copyright and, if notified, the publisher will be pleased to rectify any errors or omissions at the earliest possible opportunity.